The Passion of the Lord

FACETS

Selected Titles in the Facets Series

The Measure of a Man
Martin Luther King Jr.

The Bible and African Americans:
A Brief History
Vincent L. Wimbush

Race, Racism, and the Biblical Narratives
Cain Hope Felder

Who Is Christ for Us?
Dietrich Bonhoeffer

Reading Race, Reading the Bible
Peter T. Nash

Virtues and Values:
The African and African American Experience
Peter J. Paris

The Passion of the Lord

African American Reflections

edited by
James A. Noel
and Matthew V. Johnson

Fortress Press
Minneapolis

THE PASSION OF THE LORD
African American Reflections
Copyright © 2005 Augsburg Fortress. All rights reserved.
Except for brief quotations in critical articles or reviews, no
part of this book may be reproduced in any manner without
prior written permission from the publisher. Write: Augsburg Fortress, Box 1209, Minneapolis, MN 55440.

Cover art © James A. Noel, *Crucifixion(s)* 2004. Acrylic on
canvas board 11" x 14." This painting was created by the
co-editor during the completion of this volume as an aesthetic mode of reflecting on African Americans' experience
of Christ's crucifixion. It is available in a limited edition of
signed poster-prints.

Library of Congress Cataloging-in-Publication Data
The Passion of the Lord : African American reflections /
edited by James A. Noel, Matthew V. Johnson.
        p. cm. — (Facets)
  Includes bibliographical references.
  ISBN 978-0-8006-3730-9
  1. Jesus Christ—Passion. 2. Jesus Christ—African American
interpretations. I. Noel, James A., 1948- II. Johnson, Matthew V., 1961- III. Facets (Fortress Press)
  BT431.3.P37 2005
  232.96—dc22

Manufactured in the U.S.A.

Contents

Preface
vii

Contributors
ix

1. Lord of the Crucified
Matthew V. Johnson
1

2. Were You There?
James A. Noel
33

3. What Manner of Love?
JoAnne M. Terrell
51

4. Identifying with the Cross of Christ
Demetrius K. Williams
77

5. Womanist Passion
Karen Baker-Fletcher
111

6. Passionate Living
Rosetta E. Ross
145

**7. The Passion
and African American Pilgrimage**
Robert M. Franklin
160

Notes
175

Preface

The unique historical trajectory of African Americans has led them to find a passionate engagement and distinctive resonance with the Gospel story of the Passion of Jesus.

This brief volume explores the meaning of the Passion within the framework of African Americans' Christian consciousness, both historically and now. It marks a new attempt to rethink African American theology in light of the common practices and experience of generations of black Christians. How, it asks, does the biblical account of Jesus' death function in the religious experience of African Americans? How was it embraced and interpreted by enslaved Africans who became converted to Christianity? Inspired in part by the discussion of Mel Gibson's movie *The Passion of the Christ,* the contributors to this book explore

the profound and often overlooked significance of Christ's suffering and death and
the ways in which that story has sustained,
inspired, challenged, and confronted African
Americans. Certain vital themes emerge in
their reflections:

Passion. African American interaction
with the Christ story is deeply rooted in real,
concrete horror and terror suffered in the
Middle Passage, slavery, Jim Crow, lynchings,
and other acts of oppression.

Trauma and tragedy. The trauma of the
Middle Passage and slavery gave rise to a
tragic yet faith-filled vision of life among
African Americans.

Love. Womanist scholars show that no
matter how severe and unbearable the trauma
may have been, African American women
have asserted their humanity and also sustained the black community's humanity
through the exercise of love.

Revelation. Several of the authors helpfully
address the biblical texts themselves from an
explicitly African American perspective.

We hope these reflections shed light not
only on African American culture and Christianity but also on the perennial and universal human struggle with evil and on God's
redemptive action in Christ.

Contributors

Karen Baker-Fletcher is Associate Professor of Systematic Theology at Perkins School of Theology, Southern Methodist University, Dallas. Among her many publications is *Sisters of Dust, Sisters of Spirit: Womanist Wordings on God and Creation* (Fortress Press, 1998).

Robert M. Franklin is Presidential Distinguished Professor of Social Ethics, Candler School of Theology, Emory University, Atlanta. His *Liberating Visions* was published in 1990 and *Another Day's Journey: Black Churches Confronting the American Crisis* in 1997; both are from Fortress Press.

Matthew V. Johnson Sr. is Pastor of Christian Fellowship Baptist Church in College Park, Georgia, and holds a doctorate in philosophical theology from the University of Chicago.

James A. Noel is Associate Professor of American Religion at San Francisco Theological Seminary, San Anselmo, and Interim Pastor at Sojourner Truth Presbyterian Church, Richmond, California.

Rosetta E. Ross is Associate Professor of Religion and Chair of the Department of Religion and Philosophy at Spelman College, Atlanta. She is author of *Witnessing and Testifying: Black Women, Religion, and Civil Rights* (Fortress Press, 2003).

JoAnne M. Terrell is Associate Professor of Ethics and Theology at Chicago Theological Seminary and also Associate Pastor of Greater Walters African Methodist Episcopal Zion Church, Chicago. She is author of *Power in the Blood? The Cross in the African American Experience* (Orbis, 1998).

Demetrius K. Williams is Associate Professor in the Department of Classical Studies and Director of the Religious Studies Program at Tulane University, where he teaches New Testament, Greek, and the Bible in African American experience. He is author of *Enemies of the Cross of Christ* (2002) and *An End to This Strife: The Politics of Gender in African American Churches* (Fortress Press, 2004).

1.

Lord of the Crucified

Matthew V. Johnson

African Americans' deep engagement with
Christ's Passion has resulted in a *tragic*
expression of the Christian faith, an authentic
encounter with the reality of black suffering
without resort to escapism or denial. It has
redeemed black suffering.

During my graduate studies in the mid
1980s at the University of Chicago, I heard lectures on the history of early American Christianity by internationally renowned experts in
the field. Occasionally the conversion to and
practice of Christianity among African American slaves would be mentioned and would
be dealt with rather dismissively as merely
a variation on the theme of early American
evangelicalism. This position was not unique
to scholars at the University of Chicago. They
would point to the shared experiences of

emotionally intense forms of expression in worship, conversion accounts that emphasized inner experience or feeling as confirmation of salvation, the commonality of themes such as heaven, hell, damnation, and so forth to indicate a fundamental identity amid relative degrees of difference. The implication was of course that African American Christianity was in principle and in substance no different from other American evangelical forms. This position persisted in spite of claims made by the Black Theology movement led by James Cone,[1] Gayraud Wilmore,[2] and others that African American Christianity was fundamentally different from that of the master class in that (1) it made prominent use of African residuals and (2) the theme of liberation was (is) central to its faith and practice.[3] They cited as evidence the persistence of practices of African origin, such as the ring shout, religiously motivated rebellions, and forms of resistance; African American abolitionist writings; the pervasiveness of themes of liberation in the spirituals; and the selective emphasis on and centrality of those paradigmatic persons and stories that dealt with struggle, exile, and freedom. Among these Moses and the story of the exodus took pride of place.

Although the Black Theology movement is far closer to the truth, in point of fact, neither of these positions gives due consideration to the nature and texture of African American Christian consciousness, its distinct collective and individual quality, or its radical theological implications.[4] A focus on similarities to white evangelical expression bypasses the context in which African Americans appropriated the Christian message and what the African American brought to the table in terms of her own subjectivity and experience of selfhood. Her subjectivity was constituted within the matrix of powerful social, psychological, and cultural forces, mediated through daily experience that threatened to rip, shred, flay, or otherwise tear her apart. What the gospel became in African American Christian consciousness was determined by what it signified, the way it signified, and the particular needs for signification that drove the African American quest for wholeness. The "field" of African American experience, consisting of intricate psychological, sociological, and cultural dynamics, worked much like an oscillator through which the Christian religion was fed, producing a wave of spirituality of a particularly tragic frequency, tone, and color.

Hence, when African Americans engage the Passion of Christ—the suffering, the physical and mental exhaustion, the pain, the brutality, the collective sorrow, the abandonment, the shock, the disillusionment, the longing, and the shame—it is hardly an exaggerated display of gratuitous violence, or a dis-passionate account or recounting of a distant episode in the life of the faith. Rather, it is an all too real depiction (though not exhaustive) of the nature of life, the arbitrarily cruel and brutal violence to which the vulnerable and oppressed are subject by "legitimate" authority, the absence of any real protection under "the law," and a reflection of their ongoing, protracted inner/outer crucifixion and the thick lingering atmosphere of imminent woe. African Americans therefore occupy a distinct and, in terms of knowledge, privileged position in relation to the Passion, indeed the gospel, and the tragic mythopoetic vision it entails. They occupy this position by virtue of their equally tragic poise and existential posture. This "privileged position" was purchased not through the exchange of great ideas but by an excessive premium paid out in pain.

Jesus' Suffering and Our Own

Tragic suffering is not the exclusive possession of African Americans. Others, it is true, have passed through the Valley of Baca (Psalm 84: the valley of suffering, tears). Nevertheless, by virtue of the chronic nature of their predicament, African Americans, unlike others who passed or pass through the valley, were forced to settle there. They had no choice but to adapt to the wilderness of sorrow or perish amid its trackless wastes. It is this shared experience and collective adaptation mediated through the appropriation of the Christian faith that led to the formation of African American Christian consciousness and the emergence of a tradition of a particular nature. African Americans formed a collective communal orientation that coalesced from the mass of shared group experiences. Individuals from many different persuasions experience trauma and tragic suffering and even engage the Christian faith in their varied responses and coping strategies; here, however, is a difference in degree that culminates in a difference in kind. The formation of a *tradition* presupposes collective experience. The living repository of this tradition is the African American church. With collectively experienced trauma, not only does the body remember, as in the case of individual experiences, but the group remembers and can respond in and through group formation. The memory of these experiences takes on different appearances, among them religious expression. The experience of trauma in the case of African Americans was integral to the formation of individual and group identity and cannot easily be overestimated; in fact, it has been systematically underestimated and often overlooked in religious studies.

Some, particularly European Americans, may recoil from this notion, interpreting my thesis as a claim to a *morally* superior position for African Americans with respect to the gospel. Although that may in fact be the case, it is not the necessary implication of my view. I am claiming that their experience provides one of the most fruitful locations in modernity for doing a theology grounded in the experience of the church. Moreover, the existential recoil of European Americans to African American claims of spiritual and theological distinction have always struck me as analogous to a resentful bee angry at the flower he fertilized while robbing it. The bee would not only rob the flower but in the end begrudge it the inadvertent pollination. This, I think, is morally and intellectually reprehensible.

There is an intimate relationship between trauma and the tragic as I understand them. The Passion of Christ reflects the presence and intimate connection of both, as does African American Christian consciousness. Although one might make an argument for Buddhism, Christianity is the only one of the world's great religions whose origin, nature, and perhaps growth can be traced directly

to a *founding trauma*—the Passion of Christ,
which culminates in his brutal crucifixion
and death. This observation is much more
than incidental. What could possibly be more
of a trauma than to witness the torturous crucifixion and murder of God, the very ground
of the meaning and value of life? What tale is
more tragic than the narration of his end? The
Passion of Christ was not the unsullied victory of Moses on the seashore. Christ did not
emerge unscathed like Daniel from the lions'
den. Jesus, permanently scarred, must bear
the marks ever after. Unlike the fabled Hebrew
boys, his ordeal in the furnace of affliction
left the evidence of his trial seared into the
pigment of his skin. In a sense, Jesus' suffering answers Job's. Perhaps God's generosity
could have arranged the birth of a second set
of children to erase the pain of losing the first.
But in the aftermath of his ordeal, Job could
never return to the life he once knew. That
life with its facile trusts, shallow safeties, and
untarnished joys was gone forever, or, more
to the point, put to the lie. In the Passion of
Christ the ontological flaw of human life is
laid bear at its foundation and given mythopoetic expression that discloses its depth and
grounds it in ultimate reality. In it the veil
of human pretension is torn away, revealing
the ultimate futility of ritual remedy, while

the Passion itself becomes the framework in which Job's suffering and indeed that of all other Jobs ever after must be apprehended.

I use the phrase "theology of African American Christian consciousness" to distinguish the line of thought I am developing here from black or liberation theology. Although we have learned a lot from both, I think there are some severe methodological limitations that are fundamental to the Black Theology movement, which tends to distort African American Christian religious experience and leaves ill-analyzed some of its most salient features. I believe this flaw has limited the Black Theology movement and its usefulness in both the church and the academy. Its usefulness in the church has been minimized because its failure to understand the nature of the experience inevitably leads to a kind of alienation from the very institution it seeks to speak to and for. In the academy the movement has been limited in its effectiveness because the premature imposition of the highly politicized norm of liberation distorts the rich religious heritage of African Americans. The world can learn much from this heritage about human beings under extreme duress and the ways in which religion contributes under these conditions to the creation of a coping strategy, a vehicle of adaptation (with often ambiguous effects over the long haul), and the drive for health and healing in the face of tremendous forces of trauma, fragmentation, and psychic dismemberment. From the perspective of the theology of African American Christian consciousness, any theology based on this experience must first adequately analyze the experience on its own terms, as free as possible of any presumptively normative theological ideas such as liberation, and move on from there to a theology that adequately reflects and speaks to the consciousness of the church. I do believe that liberation is a constant theme—longing and desire expressed in the rich religious heritage of African Americans—but the secret to both its meaning and its theological grounding is not in the presence of the theme but the religious consciousness in which, through which, and by which it is expressed.

To understand the profound significance of the Passion of Christ in African American Christian consciousness, we cannot simply go to the textual expressions of highly celebrated figures in the history of the African American struggle for liberation. We must delve deeply into the experience of everyday African Americans, as they left the fields, jobs, and profane space of the inherently racist European American dominated world, both during and after slavery, and entered the context of worship. Here we will locate the profound significance of the Passion of Christ. As Jürgen Moltmann has written, "it is impossible to overlook how much this passion mysticism was and is the devotion of the poor and sick, the oppressed and crushed. The 'God' of the poor, the peasant and the slave has always been the poor, suffering, unprotected Christ, whereas, the God of empires and rulers has usually been the Pantocrator, Christ enthroned in heaven."[5] This context provides us with the advantage of a magnified view of the deep structure of African American religious and cultural consciousness and the titanic struggle going on beneath the surface to maintain psychic equilibrium and spiritual integrity in the face of a tense and deeply conflicted intersubjective reality.

To begin with, one must understand the circumstances under which African Americans encountered and appropriated the Christian faith. After the shock and trauma of the Middle Passage, where Africans were torn away from their traditional setting, they were left without access to their land and culture, including their religion and their gods, whose reality and spiritual efficacy were tied to the land and community. They were systematically stripped of their religion and culture upon coming to North America in order to protect the security and economic interests of their European American oppressors. Capture was traumatic. The holding prisons and conditions prior to being shipped were traumatic. The Middle Passage itself, where millions of African Americans perished from suicide, death by despair, disease, rape, and murder at the hands of their captors or in justifiable revolt, was a trauma of unimaginable proportions. Finally the systematic employment of brutal "slave-breaking" techniques, the object of which was to "make them stand in fear" after arriving in North America, deepened and determined the initial conditions and indeed set the tone for the lives of the African slaves and their progeny in America. Each new arrival refreshed the initial trauma for first-generation Africans and infused a diabolical vitality into the generative undercurrent of trauma that became the context for African American personhood or subjectivity.

This state of existence was further complicated by the fact that Africans were not allowed to integrate into American culture and society except on the terms established by their European American oppressors, which defined them as chattel and their character as inherently corrupt, criminal, inferior, subhuman, defiled, and a host of other traits, all of which became a part of a cultural taxonomy defining "Black Being." The drive for meaning or, as Victor Frankl has called it, the "will toward meaning"[6] gave rise to a deep need to "locate" themselves, which, in turn, precipitated a tense, deeply conflicted internalization of the cultural taxonomy and set up the conditions of inevitable endo-psychic conflict—the "sparagmous"[7] (from *sparagmos*, Greek for ritual death or dismemberment) characteristic of the tragic worldview.

This syndrome created a stressed field of being in which African Americans were threatened with psychic fragmentation. The fact that African Americans were torn away from their own land and culture and unable to settle in the one where they were physically located institutionalized their marginalization as a group along with threats of separation, loss of control over bodily integrity, daily brutality, chronic mourning, and all the other factors that configured the institutionalized terror of slavery, creating and sustaining a traumatic field in which African American Christian and cultural consciousness emerged. There was a permanent sense of homelessness in what it meant and means to be African American. In some way, then, African Americans never fully emerged from the Middle Passage: they remain still very much on the water, struggling with titanic forces that threaten their spiritual integrity.

This state of homelessness was one of the reasons that heaven became such an important symbol in the religious life of African Americans. The African American, in the Middle Passage, was suspended between two worlds. One, the African, though recollected with varying degrees of clarity and intensity at both the individual and the collective levels, ambiguously fades into the background, while the other, distant-vision America, looms ambiguously in the foreground. African Americans were then and remain today very much on the water. When adrift on great waters or on a journey in strange and uncharted seas, without the benefit of the cultural artifacts that facilitate navigation, the sky becomes the only point of stable contact, the only reliable means of navigation, a fixed reference point for a rough determination of location.

Even more than this, the navigational method in the Middle Passage, where African American humanity was stripped of all the usual instruments that facilitate movement through life, was a kind of "death reckoning," which relativized any fixed point in the here and now by an essentially entropic encounter with nothingness. Under such conditions, where there is no fixed point by which to locate, in a world where everything is thrown into question, where desire opens into nothingness and comes to rest nowhere, the human spirit undergoes dissipation. African Americans appropriated the symbol of heaven, *a place* outside of the vagaries of temporality, as the only stable reference point to mark their path on the waters. It countered and arrested the dissipation to which the human spirit is subject when its deepest desires and fundamental human aspirations have no place to rest, and the search for stable reference points to reconstruct a coherent worldview is frustrated at every turn. The symbol of heaven provided African Americans with a structure for the constitution of subjectivity and the beginnings of a new selfhood. They came to know they were somewhere between heaven and an inhospitable earth but not quite located either place. Earth faded like Africa into the background, and heaven loomed in the foreground, but unlike America it beckoned with open arms. They remained on the water, essentially out to sea and "trying to make Heaven [their] home."

This fundamental longing, of which earthly freedom was one instance and of which the centrality of heaven was the supreme manifestation, reflects the fact that African Americans were in a constant state of question with respect to earthly existence. While Martin Heidegger understands the *dasein*, or human being, to be the being who can raise the question of being,[8] to be an African American was to be the being for whom to be was to be in question. Since African Americans were never quite defined, accepted, comfortable with their identity, or sure of where or if they fit in or if they ever would, longing became an integral aspect of African American Christian consciousness.

The focus on heaven was not merely a ruse to talk about earthly freedom. It had a far richer and deeper symbolic resonance: it was a radical indictment of the world created by their oppressors and the conditions under which they were forced to live. African American *otherworldliness* was not inherently apolitical nor does it necessarily lead to a conservative political agenda. By its very nature it proclaimed their unyielding hope and their everlasting determination not to accept the prevailing conditions nor the prevailing taxonomy that sought to define black being in a way that left them eternally marred and inferior. Heaven became the unassailable repository of the hope against hope—against that day when God would move and they likewise in his train.

Faith and Meaning

What then was faith under these circumstances? Faith in the African American community was not the simplistic prattle of platitudes designed to indoctrinate the ignorant. Nor did they ever accept the pat answers of the poppy peddlers sent to placate their yearning with the time-tested opiate of religious fatalism. Faith did not provide the sure and certain answers to all their questions in the empty rationale of a four-point plan. It was something more, something far richer, deeper, and true. Faith facilitated a meaningful life in the face of unanswered questions. It empowered them to live *with* unanswered questions and amid profound existential ambiguity. It allowed them to face the reality of uncertainty in the midst of suffering without denial or escape into delusion; hence it allowed them to live as true to themselves and their God as humanly possible. In a word, it enabled them to worship in spirit and in truth—unlike much of what is now passing for spirituality in the African American church. The experience of faith is deeply grounded in what Theophus Smith refers to as the African American "wisdom tradition": "The wisdom tradition of black North American folk culture dissents from the predominant Western form of disjunctive thinking—that conventional 'either/or' in which rationalism insists on unambiguous, univocal meanings for things. Instead this tradition prefers the conjunctive 'both/and' of archaic and oral cultures, in which ambiguity and multivocity are taken for granted (even promoted)."[9]

This dimension of our experience marks off clearly for us its tragic nature, but also its authenticity. In this, as well, we see its healing power and its ability to transform the absurd in our existence into something beautiful and meaningful and into the power to "go on." The feeling of well-being is the result of the encounter with the evil and suffering in our circumstances, transfigured by the aesthetic and poetic through song and sermon. This creative, transformative power, the expression of our rudimentary hope and fundamental affirmation of the worthwhileness of life that mushroomed in what W. E. B. DuBois called the Pithian madness is captured in the familiar refrain, "I feel like going on" or, put in another vein, "I think I'll run on and see what the end will be." The encounter was mediated by the mythopoetic *mirror* of Christ's Passion, the overarching or meta-mythopoetic narrative in which all other biblical expressions in African American Christian consciousness are subsumed. Even when it is not the explicit

focal point, it is always implicit in the experience. "Because black slaves knew the significance of the pain and shame of Jesus' death
on the cross, they found themselves by his
side."[10] Christ's lordship elevated and dignified
the pain and suffering of the crucified, coun-
tering the debilitating degradation, shame,
sense of worthlessness, and abandonment. In
a word he became Lord of the Crucified. "By
his suffering and death, Jesus identified himself with those who were enslaved, and took
their pain upon himself. And if he was not
alone in his suffering, nor were they aban-
doned in the pains of their slavery. Jesus was
with them."[11]

Irene Smith Landsman's insightful article,
"Crises of Meaning in Trauma and Loss,"
helps crystallize the point I am arguing about
the traumatic nature of African American
experience and its marks on the formation of
their Christian consciousness. Her words also
clearly point to the inherent polarity of such
a consciousness:

> On the one hand, some victims confront the
> realities of existence and find them bleak.
> They see the world as without justice and feel
> unable to control their destiny. Their sche-
> mas of meaning, or world assumptions, have
> been changed, but in a way that is ultimately
> negative. Without hope, they lack even what
> Shelly Taylor has termed "positive illusions,"

and are not able to escape the pain, disappointment, and loss they have experienced—they are in despair. On the other hand, because of this existential confrontation, others are able to accept the limits of justice and control. They perceive life's fragility and their own vulnerability but find it a motivating force that makes life more meaningful. Without existential denial, they are still able to maintain hope, self-esteem, and a sense of purpose in life. Schemas or assumptions have been altered by trauma, have not been rebuilt to a pretrauma configuration, but leave room for an engagement with life and with the future. Despite a trauma and sometimes radical change to some schemas some survivors retain a sense of meaningfulness in the sense of Antonovsky's model—assumptions of nonrandomness, justice, and control may have been altered, but life continues to be found worthy of emotional investment. *And sometimes these are the same people.* While despair and transcendence are vastly different states, it may be that transcendence cannot be truly experienced without a close encounter with despair.[12] [italics mine]

The two poles are pervasive throughout the experience. There is a dialectic of hope/resignation, joy/sorrow, and suffering/celebration. They are not, however, separate states, but constitutive of one continuous field. Scholars from Howard Thurman, DuBois, and Lawrence

Levine to Lerone Bennet have remarked on the presence of the two seemingly contrary poles through which the "Negro mood" gains articulation.[13] I will let three quotations from the literature suffice to make the point. First, Lawrence Levine writes in his classic *Black Culture and Black Consciousness*:

> The religious music of the slave is almost devoid of feelings of depravity or unworthiness, but is rather, as I have tried to show, pervaded by a sense of change, transcendence, ultimate justice, and personal worth. The spirituals have been referred to as "sorrow songs," and in some respects they were. The slaves sang of "rollin thro' an unfriendly world," of being "a-troubled in de mind," of living in a world which was a "howling wilderness," "a hell to me," of "feeling like a motherless child," "a po' little orphan chile in de worl'," a "home-less child," of fearing that "Trouble will bury me down." But these feelings were rarely pervasive or permanent; almost always they were overshadowed by a triumphant note of affirmation.[14]

DuBois wrote: "The music of Negro religion is that plaintive rhythmic melody, with its touching minor cadences, which, despite caricature and defilement, still remains the most original and beautiful expression of human life and longing yet born on American soil.

Sprung from the African forests, where its counterpart can still be heard, it was adapted, changed, and intensified by the tragic soul life of the slave, until, under the stress of law and whip, it became the one true expression of a people's sorrow, despair and hope."[15] And Howard Thurman wrote of the African American spirituals, "in many ways they are the voice, sometimes strident, sometimes muted and weary, of a people for whom the cup of suffering overflowed in haunting tones of majesty, beauty and power."[16] What Friedrich Nietzsche said of the Greeks may be more aptly applied to African Americans. "What suffering must this race have endured in order to accomplish such beauty." Both the sorrow and the joy are transformed by the presence of the other as they coexist in a living tension. It is the conscious content, the mood structure, and the feeling tone of African American Christian consciousness, and it is fundamentally tragic. This contrasts sharply with the superficial joy or celebration manipulatively manufactured by the "big show" spectacle that characterizes much of the modern charismatic prosperity movement now sweeping some quarters of the African American church.

Much of the spectacle in some churches today is nothing more than a denuded imitation of African American Christian consciousness. It is what some European Americans have been telling us all along in revisionist histories of slavery and so forth: deny your pain. You are happy in your dependency and servant status in spite of its implicit inferiority. Your so-called suffering is the invention of your own unscrupulous leaders intent on preserving your victim status for their own political purposes. African American churches today, particularly those of the charismatic or prosperity stripe and those influenced by and mimicking their liturgy of manipulation, have become little more than a grotesque caricature of themselves. They project an image of Christian faith stripped of its depth and power by white evangelicals who have not shared the experience, then repackaged by their black apprentices and resold to gullible African Americans as though it were some new dispensation of the Holy Spirit.

Our forbearers had crossed too many hills and valleys, had spent too many nights in briny tears on bended knees, had seen too many dreams deferred and hopes exploded, had ridden out too many storms on the turbulent swells of wine dark seas, had sown too many seasons the sweetness of aspiration only to reap the tortured harvest of a bitter disappointment to ever deny their oppression or the integrity of their pain. In the face of their

apparent weakness, they had been carried too
often from strength to strength and in the face
of the overwhelming flood had too often risen
to the rock that David said was "higher than I."
When by sunset dreams deferred had shriveled
in the baking sun of oppression, they too often
found those same dreams revived and wet with
the dew of promise at daybreak. They had
bowed under the weight of unbearable burdens
and on bended knee called to an invisible God
and too many times rose with strength out of
an apparent nowhere, determined to "run on to
see what the end would be," to ever deny the
joy in the God of their salvation.

Crucifixion and the Tragic Vision

Martin Hengel points out clearly in his short
but powerful and painfully accurate book
Crucifixion that death by crucifixion was
widely considered the punishment of slaves
(*servile supplicium*) in the Roman Empire. It
was reserved almost exclusively for slaves,
outside of bandits, murderers, and rebellious
foreigners. The "punishment of slaves" was so
degrading that it was considered beneath a
Roman citizen, though he might be guilty of
a capital offense and receive some other form
of capital punishment. "Of course because of
its harshness, crucifixion was almost always

inflicted only on the lower class (humiliores); the upper class (honestiores) could reckon with more 'humane' punishment."[17] The imperial objective of death by crucifixion was the complete shame and degradation of the crucified. By implication it reinforced the order of domination by the horror it invoked and the distinctions it drew with respect to those on the inside and those on the "outs." As such it was intended as a deterrent for criminals, but for slaves (often with an ethnic inflection) in the Roman Empire the threat of crucifixion and its reality was a lingering, integral dynamic in their condition. Crucifixion and otherness were fundamentally connected. Jesus was crucified outside the gates of Jerusalem.

Crucifixion is reserved for those on the periphery as opposed to those at the center. African Americans were subject to an ongoing sparagmous, a shredding, a tearing apart, indeed a protracted crucifixion by virtue of the field in which they were forced to grapple with the meaning of existence. In this sense "crucifixion" resulting in physical death is the logical goal or inner logic of the condition of a slave and indeed of the oppressed as such. Fannie Lou Hamer provides an eloquent illustration of the point. Reflecting on her affirmative response to a request by James Bevel and others to go down to a Mississippi courthouse to protest during the Civil Rights Movement, she ruminated, "The only thing they could do to me was kill me, and it seemed like they'd been trying to do that a little bit at a time ever since I could remember."[18] Christ's incarnation culminating in the cross leads to a complete identification with the slave and all of humanity at its lowest and is the most concrete expression of its tragic condition.

> In the spirituals the death of Jesus took on a deep and personal poignancy. It was not merely the death of a man or a God, but there was in it a quality of identification in experience that continues to burn its way deep into the heart even of the most unemotional. The suffering of Jesus on the cross was something more. He suffered, He died, but not alone—they were with Him. They knew what He suffered; it was a cry of the heart that found a response and an echo in their own woes. They entered the fellowship of His suffering. There was something universal in His suffering, something that reached through all the levels of society and encompassed in its sweep the entire human race.[19]

The fullness of human existence is incarnated, mirrored, and absorbed in the act of God's emptying.

African Americans were forced by circumstance to engage a fundamental ontological insight incarnate in their condition—the tragic. William Storm writes:

> Far from the "metaphysical solace" that Nietzsche promises as a salutary effect of tragedy, what the tragic itself brings—and I am speaking of its unmediated, a priori condition—is metaphysical terror. The extent to which the tragic forbids such ideals as union, wholeness, or "Oneness," plus the range of rifts and bifurcations that ensure the divisions within being and between being and the world, and the utter solitude that invariably results, must finally be productive of a profound separation trauma in the beholder of such extremities. The tragic, in its pure and unrelieved state, implies a level of being that is so broken as to be untenable, and indeed unlivable.[20]

African Americans encountered and engaged the utter threat of non-being, which, translated into psychological terms, is the threat of the meaninglessness and worthlessness of existence. The conditions of their encounter with this overarching threat to their spiritual, psychic, and indeed ontological integrity were sustained by a traumatic/tragic field; this field left them scant resources to construct a coherent worldview that could sustain the basic assumptions of the value and meaning of existence, the benevolence of the world, and their self-worth. African Americans resided in a traumatic field that, unlike episodic trauma, did not allow the restoration of a static world-view, which would have preserved a revitalized form of these assumptions. They could not merely *get on* with their lives; they had to constantly *go on* with their lives. Because of the chronic nature of their ordeal, self-worth and the meaning of life and the world had to be created and sustained by an ongoing effort. Nevertheless, while involved in this work, African Americans maintained a perspective on reality that allowed for what ultimately could not be denied.

Hence, they developed perhaps unconsciously a tragic vision of the gospel whose central theme was the Passion of Christ, which thus became the metanarrative in which African American Christian consciousness took shape. Their tragic predicament resonated with the Passion of Christ at the point of the tragic, reflecting a basic ontological disturbance. This is the nexus on which an authentically African American theology must be constructed, a theology true to the gospel and true to the experience. I am arguing here that there is a fundamental congruity among African American Christian consciousness, the gospel of

Christ—understood through the core criterion of the Passion—and ontology. African American theology has a message not simply *for* African Americans but *from* African Americans to the whole of the Christian church and the world.

Finally, a word about revelation as a religious experience and its place in African American Christian consciousness: The rather familiar descriptions of conversion experiences, rich in detail and spiritual integrity, and the traditionally conservative language used by African Americans to describe their faith should not be confused with either the essence or the sum total of its meaning.[21] They provide merely the gateway to a deeper spiritual experience with stunning theological implications. However individualistic the language of confession seems, conversion always took place within the context of the rich communal experience. Read this way, it becomes relatively transparent that the necessary components for the formation of coherent selfhood—mirroring, twinship, and idealization—are wrapped up in the polyvalent experience of the transfigured communal context of worship. Charles Strozier writes of Heinz Kohut that he "feels that religion satisfies twinship needs in the locale of the church or the sacred environment and especially in one's participation in the congregation. Religion, of course, is both a solitary and a communal experience. Much of what religion does in meeting idealizing and mirroring needs is solitary: Something goes on in private between you and your concept of God. But religion is also communal. Church surrounds you with worshippers like yourself who have made common faith commitments."[22]

Yet even when not assembled, the communal reality inheres in the intersubjective subset of alternative meanings that formed the slave community's alternate spiritual world—a world validated only in and through their shared experiences. The revelation of Christ was always already mediated in and through the community. Hence revelation always implies the community and cannot be conceived in any theology grounded in African American Christian consciousness outside of that context. Christ lives in and amid the community and indeed is the community, and as such his broken body mediates grace and wholeness. Strozier writes, "Such mirroring needs, Kohut says, are met in religion through what is usually called grace or the idea that 'there is something given to you, some innate perception of your right to be here and to assert yourself, and that somebody will smile at you and will respond to you and will be in turn with your worthwhileness.'"[23]

I have been arguing the central significance of the Passion of Christ as the metanarrative of African American Christian consciousness. Here I must qualify the centrality of the Passion by combining it with a field interpretation of the gospel and as the core of the gospel. This field interpretation is consistent with and suggested by African American Christian consciousness. "Similarly, the piety of the Negro spirituals sung by black slaves in the southern states of the USA concentrates upon the crucifixion *and* resurrection of Jesus"[24] (italics mine).

We are used to thinking of the Passion narratives and the resurrection narratives in sequential or linear terms. Yet what is seen in narrative's *linear* chronology as death and resurrection becomes at once present in the mythopoetic mediation of the passion/resurrection. Chronology is the limitation of narrative, but the mythopoetic whole embedded in the narrative is the revelation of being and the Divine in its fullness. In describing how the field model works in the context of literary theory, N. Katherine Hayles uses the example of "'reversible' drawings that psychologists call equivocal figures."[25] "It is apparent that one's mindset, rather than the picture itself, determines which figure is primary. Because neither could exist without the other, to designate either as ground or

figure is arbitrary; they mutually define each
other. The relevant point is that human cogni-
tion is such that only one figure can be brought
into focus at a time, even though we know that
they are interconnected."[26]

The revelation of Christ's meaning is
encountered in much the way Hayles describes
the reader's engagement of Thomas Pyn-
chon's *Gravity's Rainbow*. "The difference in
perspective arises because in *Gravity's Rainbow* meaning arrives as a *gestalt*, precipitat-
ing into awareness; either one sees the whole
design, or one doesn't see it at all. For those
that do, the technique forges a bridge between
the emerging sense of a field view and the
experience of reading [read *revelation*]. The
very fact that we can see the connections
means that we are participating in the mode
of vision being described. *Gravity's Rainbow*
is thus both a narrative and an initiation [read
conversion]."[27] God is ever crucified, yet ever,
always overcoming. He is the ever-crucified,
life-affirming power. One may ask at this
point, Does God then have any real option for
the poor and the broken in the Christian revelation? He certainly does. They are the most
likely to see and receive it.

An authentic Christian spirituality such
as we witness in traditional African American Christian consciousness is not the glib,

shallow, clinically sanitized, often greedy and rapacious triumphalism we see in so much traditional Western theology and praxis, which relies on an anti-tragic hermeneutic. It is rather a deep and abiding affirmation of life always already amid its *sparagmos*—its torn, tense, often shredded and conflicted nature. It is close if not identical to what Nietzsche referred to as the "pessimism of strength" as articulated by Pfeffer in her classic work, *Nietzsche: Disciple of Dionysus*. It is the orientation to the world that Nietzsche argues is the manifest consciousness of the tragic human subject, the modus vivendi of the Dionysian spirit, the "deep that calls unto deep." "It is a call not from above, but from the depth of the abyss and the anguish of our inner consciousness to face the absurdity of the human condition, the desert and 'wasteland' around us, and transform it into a 'fruitful farmland'—into a new tragic religion that affirms the totality of life 'with all that is greatest and all that is smallest' and deems it holy."[28] The tragic subject sees reality for what it is but in the midst of it affirms life's value out of its depth, ever overcoming through creativity and the transfiguring powers of beauty.

2.

Were You There?

James A. Noel

> O sometimes it causes me to tremble. . . .
> Were you there when they crucified my
> Lord?
> —Negro spiritual

Mel Gibson's *The Passion of the Christ* pro-voked a tremendous amount of debate, particularly among religious viewers. For the most part, white evangelical Protestants and Roman Catholics liked the movie, while white liberal Protestants and Jews disliked it. Black Christians were rarely brought into the discussion in any meaningful way, since whites were the only acknowledged adjudicators of the questions of Christ and salvation raised by the film. In fact, most African Americans, in opposition to their white liberal Protestant counterparts, with whom they agree on many social issues, liked the movie. In exploring the reasons why, I will focus on the central role played by Christ's Passion in the African American religious imagination.

Where Is the Passion?

Historically, white liberal Protestants embraced modernity in such a way that made them uncomfortable with theological language about the efficacious nature of Jesus' crucifixion and death. White evangelicals, on the other hand, responded to modernity in such a way that allowed them to retain the traditional language and conceptualization of the Atonement. Black people were not ushered into modernity through the Protestant Reformation and the European Enlightenment but through their underside—slavery. Thus Passion piety survives among two constituencies within American Protestantism that are at serious odds on issues of racial equality and social justice. African Americans view white evangelicals as politically conservative and racist. So what would explain this apparent common identity in the piety of these two groups? First, we must note that African Americans were not involved in the modernist-fundamentalist controversy. Prior to this controversy, how-

ever, African Americans were the objects of
the debate over slavery.

The slavery debate heated up during the
1830s and took on a different tenor and intensity when Southerners went on the offensive.
They no longer merely defended the "peculiar institution" from abolitionist critiques
but made pro-slavery arguments that were
buttressed with numerous proof texts from
the Bible. The Southerners would have had
the rhetorical advantage in such arguments
if both parties were confined to literal readings of the Bible. However, the higher critical
methods of biblical interpretation developed
in Germany had reached the United States
through people like Albert Barnes, a professor of Old Testament at Union Theological Seminary. Abolitionists found that they
could counter the pro-slavery advocates' use
of texts that supported slavery by using the
tools of higher criticism to disclose the overarching theme of salvation history and the
gospel. When hostilities broke out between
the North and the South, both sides were convinced that God was championing their cause.
The North's victory vindicated its theological
interpretation of the conflict and inflicted a
serious wound on the Southern psyche. As a
defensive maneuver, Southerners interpreted
their defeat to mean not that their cause had

been opposed to God's will but that they were the victims of the godless Northerners and "bestial" blacks. The symbol of the cross retained its potency within this psychological paradigm. It is no coincidence that the main organization that emerged for the purpose of intimidating blacks through racial violence and murder, the Ku Klux Klan, would signify its presence through cross burnings.

The South's racial mind-set had inculcated an anti-intellectualism into its ethos. The Southern mind repressed free inquiry and curiosity lest it lead the inquirer to conclusions falling outside approved social convention. The Scopes Trial dramatically portrayed the Southern flight from modernity. As the victor in the Civil War, the North exercised cultural hegemony over the nation, and northern liberals enjoyed greater social prestige than their evangelical counterparts. As the liberals embraced modernism, privileging scientific methods and achievements over traditional, often religiously based views, theological language about the efficacious nature of Jesus' death became unintelligible to them. Liberal Protestant clergy were unable to help their modernist congregations engage with the spiritual significance of Jesus' crucifixion.

The Social Gospel was a major movement in the liberal wing of Protestantism. Its emphasis on the social ethical implications of Christian doctrines reinforced the tendency already at work in liberal Protestantism to de-emphasize the importance of belief and "undercut the relevance of the message of salvation through trust in Christ's atoning work."[1] Walter Rauschenbusch said, for example, that "religious morality" is "the only thing God cares about."[2] The evangelical wing of Protestantism reacted to the Social Gospel by moving even further away from social justice concerns.

Thus the correlations among white Protestants between Passion piety and political conservatism and the absence of such a piety and social activism can be traced back to these developments. This correlation cannot be made, however, in the case of African American Christians.

Religious Imagination

The "religious imagination" is another way of approaching the problematic concept of "religious experience." In trying to think about religious experience, we encounter the problem of not being able to gain immediate access to this phenomenon because any descriptions or ideational constructs are temporally and existentially removed from the actuality of the experience itself, which remains shrouded in silence and mystery. From that realm it carries over into the imagination, where its lingering forms glow but can only be expressed in symbols and rituals. Theological categories are yet further removed from the primal moment of ineffability wherein the initial religious experience occurred. Rudolf Otto elaborated on this point in *The Idea of the Holy*,[3] and it is also the basic presupposition of the work of the father of modern theology, Friederich Schleiermacher.

The spiritual "Were You There?" expresses an African American aesthetic mode of religious apprehension wherein Christ's Passion is the central image or symbol. African slaves took what was salvageable from their past and reinterpreted it through its amalgamation with the only other religious system available—Christianity—to develop a black Protestant faith tradition. What eventually commanded their attention as they desperately sought a compass to orient themselves and make sense of the terror they were to experience in their new land was Christ's Passion. Slaves did not apprehend this symbol through creed or doctrinal statements but through an aesthetic mode that made their lives contemporaneous with that event. "Were You There?" should be seen as an expression of the African American slave's aesthetic mode of religious apprehension: singing it was a performative ritual that situated them at the foot of the cross, where they gained insight into the theology of the cross.

The painting I made for this book's cover is my attempt to capture this idea visually. My intent was to represent what Africans might have imagined as they sang, "Were you there when they crucified my Lord?" This painting should be viewed as the image that the slaves were constructing when they sang that song and also as the antecedent image that the song was referencing. In my conception, the slaves would have produced such an image had they enjoyed the luxury of being able to paint. My inspiration came from several crucifixion scenes painted by William H. Johnson during the 1940s—particularly *Jesus and the Three Marys* (ca. 1939–40), *Mount Calvary* (ca. 1944), and *Lamentation/Descent from the Cross* (ca. 1944). One of Johnson's foremost concerns was his desire to render through his paintings an accurate visual depiction of the African American experience. This concern had been central to the artistic endeavors of African American visual and literary artists from the time of the Harlem Renaissance forward and had served as a sort of manifesto. Although Johnson had been academically trained in his craft, he found that he had to abandon many of the academic rules and conventions to appropriately capture the experience of being black in America. Therefore he made the conscious choice to adopt a folk style of painting to capture what "the folk" typically do, including worship. Johnson's paintings did more than merely depict African Americans in worship settings: he captured the mood and modality of their religious experience by situating the religious object in its social context. His crucifixion scenes thus show how important Christ's Passion has been to the African American religious imagination and aesthetic.

Regarding the aforementioned paintings, art historian Richard Powell described them as "a brilliant, Afrocentric folk version of the crucifixion." According to Powell, the material Johnson drew upon for his depiction of the crucifixion was as broad as Matthias Grünwald's *The Crucifixion of Christ* (ca. 1510–1515) and lynchings of African Americans in the United States. I studied Johnson's depictions of the crucifixion to develop my own image because his paintings convey a fundamental insight into an essential characteristic of African American religion. Powell writes, "As in all of Johnson's black interpretations of Christian themes, the raised arms and genuflecting postures of his figures reenact an eloquent, spiritual gesture closely identified with black religious expression." In Johnson's sensibility this expression or gesture "was emblematic of African American religion."[4] This gesture is also seen in Johnson's painting *Lynch Mob Victim* (ca. 1939), in which the victim is hanging from a tree but, curiously, his hands are outstretched as if he has been nailed to a cross. In my depiction of the crucifixion I reverse the trope by draping the figures over the cross in such a way as to signify their being hung by a rope from a tree. Indeed, the two figures being crucified with Christ do not have their hands nailed to the cross at all. The roots of all three crosses actually grow into the ground, adding to the depiction of the crosses as trees. In my painting Mary's gesture beneath the cross is the one Powell saw as "emblematic of African American religion" in Johnson's paintings. Her central placement in the painting implies that she is lifting up her arms in grief over the cruel and violent deaths suffered by all three figures—not just Jesus. All three of the crucified are her boys, and because of her love for these boys—her sons—she also is undergoing crucifixion. Mary's gesture expresses her wish to take all her boys down from the cross or to die in their place. The sun will set, and she will be condemned to endure the weight of her grief. During the long days and nights that lie ahead, she will beseechingly lift up her arms to God in the same gesture.

The Spiritual "Were You There?"

The way African Americans imagine the Passion of Christ is due to the peculiarly traumatic nature of their historical experience, especially their experiences of the Middle Passage and slavery. One of the few eyewitness accounts by an African of what that voyage was like was written in 1789 by Olaudah Equiano. In his autobiography he described how during the voyage "the air soon became unfit for respiration, from a variety of loathsome smells, and brought a sickness among the slaves, of which, many died. . . . The shrieks of the women, and the groans of the dying, rendered it a scene almost inconceivable."[5] Approximately twelve million Africans were transported across the Atlantic in this way to work the sugar, tobacco, and coffee plantations in the various colonies Europeans established in the New World.

Once they arrived on North American shores, Africans had to begin to make the long adjustment that would result in an African American identity, and their conversion to Christianity was integral to this process.[6] Slaves could never adjust entirely to their experience, however, without succumbing to complete dehumanization. Adjustment, therefore, was not synonymous with accommodation. Nor was resistance synonymous with rebellion. As Howard Thurman explained in *Jesus and the Disinherited*, most slaves sought physical, psychic, and spiritual survival while suffering on all three of these fronts.[7] Physical and psychic survival hinged ultimately on the slave's ability to survive spiritually, and the slave used whatever resources were available from the African and Christian traditions to achieve this. By no means passive recipients of the new faith, they actively participated in its reception and interpretation.

Southern slave masters initially had strong reservations against allowing contact between their slaves and Christian missionaries because they rightly suspected that this would lead, either directly or indirectly, to insubordination and insurrection. White missionaries found it necessary, therefore, to give assurances to the plantation owners that their preaching would not lead to this undesirable outcome. Indeed, many missionaries took great pains to construct catechisms specifically designed to reinforce slaves' accommodation to their servile status by emphasizing and privileging biblical texts that seemed to condone slavery and admonish slaves into obedience. Paul's letters were readily put to this use, but that strategy backfired—there were aspects of Paul's writings that subverted the slave master's hermeneutic. Moreover, since a significant number of slaves attended the same church services as their masters, they were able to hear and develop their own hermeneutic regarding a broader range of texts than those that were merely designed to admonish them and force them into obedience. This was especially the case in the early nineteenth century during the Second Great Awakening, when large numbers of African Americans were exposed to the gospel. Regardless of the ethical teachings the missionaries tried to impose on the minds of their black converts, those teachings had to be based on the basic belief in Jesus' death and resurrection. This belief was encouraged through the telling of the story and not through the presentation of theological doctrines. Slaves rarely possessed Bibles that could be the basis for studying the message of the gospel. Most slaves were illiterate and had to comprehend the nature of the gospel through their encounter with the Word that was preached, prayed, and sung.

There were no rational answers to the questions that must have loomed large in their collective consciousness: Why did they have to suffer? Who ordained it? Was it deserved? They fixed their attention on the image of God choosing to enter into the very depths of their tragic condition to share their fate, which was crucifixion. This was an aesthetic perception of their reality, and perhaps all reality's super-sensuous substrate—the Infinite appearing in the finitude of suffering and death. It was not an answer to the great theodicy question at the rational level, but it was a balm and con-solation at the ontological level.

The blacks who were being crucified asked, "Were you there when they crucified my Lord?" Because they said "my Lord," it is obvious that their conversion to Christianity had already taken place. The Crucified One they sang about is also their Lord.

The lyrics of the spirituals were taken from other Christian hymns, biblical verses, and ser-mons, which were combined and improvised upon to express and invoke the collective mood of those who sang them. The spiritual was a patchwork quilt, each of whose parts was multivalent. Not all the spirituals were sorrow songs; some of them were shouted and expressed the joy the slaves experienced when under the influence of the Holy Spirit. But some spirituals did ponder the mystery of human suffering and brought the singers to that intersection of the human and divine, whose perception results in trembling. A white journalist described the sermon he heard a black minister preach behind Union lines during the Civil War: "He spoke of the 'rugged wood of the cross,' whereunto the Savior was nailed; and, after describing that scene with such power as I have ever known an orator to exhibit, he reached the climax, when he pictured the earthquake which rent the veil of the temple, with this extremely beautiful expression: 'And, my friends, the earth was unable to endure the tremendous sacrilege, and trembled.' He held his rude audience with most perfect control; subdued them, excited them, and, in fact, did what he pleased with them."[8] We can imagine the escaped slave who attended that revival later invoking the memory of that occasion and the content of the message through his or her spontaneous composition of the spiritual "Were You There?" There is no way for us to reconstruct how the song was composed, but the relationship between the content of the sermon and the song's lyrics demonstrates the interwoven nature of the relationship in slave community among worship and conversion experience, religious imagination, and lyrical composition.

"Were You There?" is a detailed meditation on Jesus' death. It asks, "Were you there when they nailed him to the cross?" "Were you there when they pierced him in the side?" "Were you there when they laid him in the tomb?" Between each of these inquiries we hear the refrain: "O sometimes it causes me to tremble, tremble, tremble; were you there when they crucified my Lord?" They trembled because they were contemplating something horrific! And they trembled because the crucifixion mirrored their historical experience.

The slaves also trembled because they sensed something inherent in the Gospels that was quite apparent to them because of their social location—the scandal of the crucifixion. In his book on the doctrine of the Atonement, Martin Hengel claims that there is no way to overstress the offensive nature of the term *crucified* that Mark uses in his Gospel in reference to Jesus. He uses the term eight times between 15:13 and 16:6. Hengel points out that the double invitation made by the leaders of the people for Jesus to come down from the cross in Mark 15:30-32 was "an appeal to transform the scandalous and accursed death into a triumph."[9]

This is the Messiah dying like us? Slavery was a scandal, and Jesus' death like a slave was also a scandal. The apprehension of God in the center of this reality was the slave's experience of what Rudolf Otto called the

"*mysterium tremendum*" and also the "sub-
lime." One could only tremble before this
epiphany! African Americans continued to
tremble even after slavery had ended.

Between 1863 and 1963 over three thousand
black people were lynched. The perpetrators
didn't just hang the victim—he or she would
be brutalized (if male castrated), hanged, and
then burned. Then after it all was over, the
perpetrators would pose before the burnt victim for a photo shoot that would be made
into postcards. In other words, lynching was
a cultural phenomenon in the United States.
Many of the people I worship with and preach
to every Sunday know about this firsthand.
One of the more well-known lynching inci-
dents was of Emmett Louis Till, a youth who
was brutally beaten and lynched for allegedly
whistling at a white woman. The perpetrators
of this form of violence boasted and glorified
their deeds through postcards, but depictions
of violence are not always equivalent to its
glorification. His body was so deformed from
the beating that the undertakers wanted to
have a closed casket. But Emmett's mother said
she wanted an open casket so that "the world
[could] see what they did to my boy."[10] Photo-
graphs of Emmett Till's open casket appeared
across the country and served to galvanize
protests led by the NAACP, the Brotherhood

of Sleeping Car Porters, and major African American leaders.

"Were you there when they crucified my Lord?" is a rhetorical question. When addressed to white America, the answer is: you are already there. Christ is present in the people you work to death, rape, whip, and lynch. The crucifixion is taking place right before your eyes, in your own time, through the system of racial exploitation that you uphold. However, white America was prevented from contemplating Christ's crucifixion with the same seriousness and intensity as African American Christians because it participated in this evil. For the slave, the crucifixion, with all its horror, was a central focus of their theological gaze. Their insight was identical to Martin Luther's, who perceived God doing something entirely new and unheard of in Christ.[11]

The Passion and Black Theology

Following the Civil War, Southern whites continued to reject higher critical approaches to biblical interpretation, Darwinism, and racial justice for the freed slaves. Liberal whites continued to embrace modernity and advocated the Social Gospel. White Protestantism became divided between liberals and fundamentalists. Liberal Protestantism did not lose its confidence until the Neo-Orthodox movement appeared after World War II, and even that was more of a critique within the liberal Protestant camp than criticism from the outside. Meanwhile, black theology and Latin American liberation theology got their start in the liberal theology academy during the Black Power movement of the late 1960s. The concerns and methods of that theology reflect its immediate and broader intellectual and social contexts.

Because black liberation theologians have not paid close enough attention to the importance of the Passion in the slave's religious experience, they have missed their opportunity to bridge the gap between their focus on racial justice and the discursive practices, symbols, and rituals still extant in the black church that grow out of the aesthetic mode focused on the cross. African American slaves discerned the symbolic reality of the cross in their spirituals and, through conversion, were enabled to survive, resist, and struggle on. Understanding the role played in the African American religious experience by religious imagination and the aesthetic mode of religious apprehension will help black theology better serve its community.

3.

What Manner of Love?

JoAnne M. Terrell

King of my life, I crown Thee now
Thine shall the glory be;
Lest I forget Thy thorn-crowned brow,
Lead me to Calvary.

Lest I forget Gethsemane;
Lest I forget Thine agony;
Lest I forget Thy love for me—
Lead me to Calvary.
                    —Jennie Evelyn Hussey[1]

The first time I attempted to see *The Passion of the Christ*, I stood in a long line among many lines for the same movie, only to have all theaters sold out the very moment I reached the front of the line. It was to good advantage that I had waited, however, because it was the first time I had ever seen so many elderly black women at a movie! In a way, I thought, this is good, because here is anecdotal evidence that they in fact value the story, even as thin a slice as Gibson had prepared. As I stood there, I mused, "What manner of love would make them come and see a depiction of the suffering and death of a God/man?" The next day, after viewing the movie, my recovery from its effect on me not quite complete, I said to myself, "Well, maybe it isn't love after all. Maybe it is just a neurotic attachment to pain." But my scornful assessment didn't quite sit right with me, because a woman in her sixties or seventies left the movie in tears and did not return. I kept nodding off during the lengthy flogging scene. I was unashamedly bored with it because I knew, like many and probably most of the people in the theater, the *end* of the story. As an African Methodist, proudly situated in the "apostolic succession," I owned my kinship to the Gospel writers, who, to an author, give away the end of the story before it is barely under way! As a progeny of slaves, I didn't need the movie so I could be "there when they crucified my Lord." I didn't have a chance to ask the woman why she had left, but I wondered if it was her sense of complicity in the violence against Jesus, and the thought just wasn't compelling to me.

I wondered what violence she had witnessed in her black person, against her black children or her sister-friends, or against her husband or any of the men in her life, and if, looking at the suffering as a mirror to her own, she could bear to look no longer.

I stayed, I think, because I am a professional theologian, a scholar, and Jesus is singularly important to me, enough for me to stick around and see what others were saying about him. I stayed because I am a Christian preacher, and as such, I *love* to tell the story, I *love* to hear it, and I know firsthand the redemptive value that a single slice of it—that even a *taste* of it—can yield to those who are waiting to hear words of comfort or of God's extravagant grace. Moreover, as Ps. 68:11 states, "The Lord gives the command; great is the company of those who bore the tidings." "Great" does not imply perfect, so, attending the movie, I did not expect, nor did I get, nor have I ever gotten, for that matter, the perfect sermon or discourse on the significance of Christ Jesus' life, suffering, and death. I certainly did not expect Hollywood to come through in this way, and, frankly, I saw the movie as yet another attempt to pass Jesus off as a white man, an image that many people of all races take for granted is the "correct" one. It is, of course, the image with which I grew up and that I now find I must resist, since it continues both to live in and limit my imagination. Director Gibson overcame his problems of translation through the use of subtitles, by relying on the familiarity of the story and the "usual" depictions. But the critique of the "imago whiteness" is a screen that people of color have to employ quite consciously in order to affirm our nontangential place in the story.

Love and Redemption

The imago whiteness notwithstanding, I stayed—I endured the movie—because I am a believer in the whole story of and about Christ Jesus as given in Scripture. It is after all the whole story of and about him that makes *me* whole. Christ Jesus is for me the complete Redeemer: God incarnate, who regularly ransoms me; who continuously satisfies a debt of honor I cannot pay; who through the record of his deeds provides a supreme moral example; who, by grace, imputes to me righteousness I have not the hope of obtaining through my efforts alone; and who, as an embattled God on the side of the oppressed, teaches me the art and means of spiritual warfare and gives me the sure hope of victory over the principalities and powers that thwart my existence, having no motive other than sheer love. In short, my prima facie reason for seeing and enduring *The Passion of the Christ* is that I simply *love* Jesus, "because," as the nineteenth-century hymnodist Frederick Whitfield said, "he first loved me."[2] I believe this is true for the many thousands of black church folks (and others) who braved the lines and contributed mightily to the material success of the film. I believe this is true whether or not they are able to recognize the influence of the theories of Origen, Anselm, Peter Abelard, Martin Luther, and Gustaf Aulén on their christological perspectives.

As for other Christians, the ransom, satisfaction, moral influence, substitution, and *Christus victor* models of the Atonement find their way into the black religious mind-set by osmosis, by way of hymns and inconsistent sermons, and through the recounting of these, many people claim to have an exhaustive understanding of the significance of the story of Christ Jesus' coming, his life and death. These theories were shaped in particular contexts and are therefore limited in their ability to inform us who do not have the same historical, cultural, religious, scientific, social, economic, and political points of reference available to the theorists.[3] Still, there is merit in attempting to understand what they were trying, despite their limitations, to give as a permanent bequest to Christians. There is merit in trying to ascertain not only what makes the central story relevant but also what makes its historical interpretations—come down to us in a complex, sometimes confused, web of scripture and tradition—compelling to contemporary generations of confessing saints. That Christ Jesus, in the lessons of his life and death, redeems and rescues us from our most unyielding adversaries (a host that almost certainly includes ourselves, never mind the Devil!); that God deserves honor, the best of what we are and think and have and do; that Jesus' life of sacramental love is exemplary; that Jesus is God, whose death for us, construed as a sacrifice made on our behalf, points most consistently to the righteousness of God and not to our own; and that we are promised victory against hidden agencies and powers are insights that must not be lost if we who belong to God and are called by Christ are to live in hope. In our liberal, positive regard for humanity, it is tempting to forget that *hopeless* people come to faith and particularly faith in Jesus because they are actually, existentially torn by having personally "missed the mark" as well as by living, suffering, and dying in a world itself torn by racism, sexism, class oppression, and war. It is therefore quite possible that the elderly black woman who left in tears left convinced of her sinfulness or that of the world or both. The best of evangelical faith proffers us power to live, that accrues by both personal and corporate awareness of an infinite, unconditional love for us, regardless. For the community of believers, Christianity is thus uniquely the religion of the "second chance" that makes our subsequent moral choices enlightened ones. Failing this, we who are Christians have the blessed assurance of "the grace of the Lord Jesus Christ, the love of God, and the communion of the Holy Spirit" (2 Cor. 13:13)[4] to sustain, inspire, forgive, educate, and keep company with us on our journey back to our origins in infinity. This is why to evangelical Christians, especially black people, "it is so *sweet* to be saved."[5]

Yet black faith, while rooted in and responsive to the evangelical impulses of American civil religion, is tempered to varying degrees by our historic struggle against slavery and by our need to continue the fight—even unto death—against racism and discrimination. For black Christians, both the Bible and experience attest to the complete redemption wrought in Christ Jesus, whose affirming, transforming touch is felt in the body, mind, and heart and makes a recognizable difference in what we do, not merely inciting us to love the One who is the king of love and sovereign of our lives, but also giving us an ethical mandate to "love the neighbor," even those enemies of our humanity.

Christian thinkers—both from within and outside black Christendom—attest to the persistence of a love ethic among African Americans.[6] In America, white slaveholders and churchmen exploited this will to love in the establishment of the slave state, brutalizing blacks while shielding themselves from social, political, and economic reprisals with a command to love and obey them, on the authority of scripture. Historically, the love ethic has entailed a willingness to sacrifice, to forgive, to forgo vengeance, and to forsake violence as a way of life.

Unlike those who see in this a sign of racial weakness,[7] I believe that possessing or, rather, being possessed *by* the will to love has functioned psychologically and spiritually to give black people a chance to reclaim our humanity, dignity, agency, and connection to God in a social context that denied us the privilege of being regarded and regarding ourselves as human beings. That said, the power and sway of the love ethic did not prevent the predominantly Christian black community, with whites and other people of goodwill, from seeking and striving for legal and political solutions to slavery and the brutality and discrimination that followed it. Indeed, the love ethic created a range of responses that issued forth in the abolitionist and Civil Rights Movements, as well as various nationalistic movements that served both to orient the love ethic toward the community itself and espouse self-defense as a human right. Exercising the right of self-defense in no way reflects on the capacity to love others or bespeaks a commitment to violence as a way of life. Rather, it demonstrates regard for the gift of one's own life, or for that of one's family, or for that of one's community of accountability.

Black liberation theologians allow that, to the extent that black people are infused with such purpose, responsibility, love of self, and the knowledge of the love of God *for us* in Christ Jesus, our redemption, our liberation, is at hand. The whole story of and about Jesus—his birth and family of origin, his life, spirituality, ministry, political activity, suffering, death, resurrection, and continuous intercession for us—provides the "soul" necessary for liberation precisely because it makes so many points of contact with our collective story. Whether or not we formally acknowledge this insight of James Cone[8] and other black theologians, together we have recognized Christ Jesus' whole story as *the* template for purposeful, responsible living, with the empowerment of love and hope beyond social and economic oppression, beyond the too-often, too-early graves that are our lot through the burdens of systemic racism, our general lack of access to health care, and the violence of the oppressive, imploding macro- and micro-cultures that are around and within us. Christ Jesus offers us the opportunity to be born anew, to be baptized into a consciousness that reflects our accountability to the just, loving requirements of our God and points to our hope for their fulfillment. And so it is Christ Jesus, whose divine significance, authority, and identity are exponentially charged in African American Christian faith and worship, who, in every way, "will be our guide"—and our *God* forever and ever—"even unto death."[9]

Love and Sacrifice

Just as it was and is incumbent upon black men and women to fight slavery and now racial discrimination with every resource at our disposal, including our faith in Christ Jesus, it was and remains necessary for women, black women in particular, to fight sexism, racism, and class oppression with all the resources at our disposal, particularly our faith. The lesson to be learned from black liberation theologians and the fruitful application of the love ethic in and beyond slavery is that, although these social evils principally characterize our experience in this context, women do not have to be defined by them. Christian men—white men and black men alike—can and do exploit the sacrificial thrust of scripture and women's will to love in their arrogated and accrued ecclesial and social power, commanding women to "keep silence" in the churches and wives to be "submissive" to their husbands even if they are mentally, emotionally, fiscally, or physically abusive. White women, as well as other women who are higher up in the color-caste system and who have more financial means, have exercised their racial and class privilege over black women and maintain this option within the hierarchy of social relations. But as heirs of the enlightenment, salvation, and liberation of Christ Jesus; as principals in both the African American and women's struggle for justice; in the light of our hard-fought-for civil and human rights, black Christian women have now the responsibility to appropriate Christ Jesus' story freshly and to be empowered by it to fight against the mind-numbing, soul-killing, murderous instincts of patriarchy-driven, racist, class-bound, violence-prone persons and systems.

Rather than merely reflect these basest of values as elements of the story, Gibson played into them by using a woman actor to portray the Devil, by letting stand as fact the scripturally unfounded implication that Mary Magdalene was the woman caught in adultery, by thoroughly implicating "the Jews" (not the Jewish leaders) and absolving the Romans in the scourging and death of Jesus, and by elevating the imago whiteness as the racial standard of the first century. Even Simon of Cyrene, the one person whom whites had for a long time generally conceded was black (perhaps because his role in helping Jesus to bear his cross helped early catechizers explain black subservience), is ethnically ambiguous and pointedly called "Jew" in the film. This is disingenuous at best because it deflects attention from the proximity of Palestine to Africa; the fact that the ancient Hebrews were people of color colonized in Egypt by another people of color; the fact that there were many more than one or two black-skinned African Jews since *before* the first century; and the fact that white-skinned Jews migrated to Palestine/ Israel from Eastern Europe in relatively recent times.[10] At worst this glaze-over of Simon's African identity says of and to black people that we have little or no historical investment in his or Jesus' story, even if we can liken the "coerced surrogacy"[11] of their situations to our own suffering. And if the news media can be trusted, it is certain that we as a people have little to add to the public discourse today about what is perhaps the most significant narrative of Western history (because it provides the backdrop for the common universe of meaning in the culture now dominating the world).

As surely as "in Christ God was reconciling the world to himself . . . and entrusting the message of reconciliation to us" (2 Cor. 5:19a), then committed Christians, that is, disciples of Christ Jesus, are to be engaged in the work of thoroughly supplanting the values of our divided world. We can do this by revisiting our ideas, discovering the fallacies and injustices therein, and changing our habits of defining others in ways that divide the world by gender, skin color, social class, sexual orientation, religion, age, weight, hair texture, nose shape, and an array of arbitrary yet culturally reinforced distinctions. Accepting that "thinking is a form of prayer,"[12] the call to committed discipleship is not a call to blind acceptance of anything. It is rather a call to prayerful rethinking of our relationship to scriptures and traditions, studying theology, history, and geography (!), and recharging our imaginations concerning histories and cultures to produce more faithful renderings thereof, to the end that we more faithfully signify the God of love who created and called us.

Black Christian women embody the ambiguity of black identity and black faith, which is paradoxically evangelical and political, reactionary and revolutionary, seeking to be faithful to the God they have encountered in scripture and experience. Womanist theologians have an ever-widening commitment to love with justice as the correct signifier of who God in Christ is and what God in Christ requires of those of us "who have not been considered disciples"[13] in the eyes of the church and society. Particularly in places that value neither blackness nor femaleness, for many of us, matters of the heart—that is, of love and our desire to give and receive it—matter most, and so a most natural starting place for theological reflection has been the story of Christ Jesus,[14] billed as a love story from "before the foundation of the world,"[15] according to our Scripture and tradition: "For God so loved the world . . ." (John 3:16). In directly addressing the person and work of Christ Jesus, in our pursuit of love with justice for our people and ourselves, womanist theologians have effectively exclaimed, along with the epistle writer: In the gift of Christ Jesus, "what manner of love the Father has bestowed on *us*, that we [too] should be called the children of God!" (1 John 3:1, NKJV).

With black theologians and other disciples, womanists consider the standards of discipleship that flow from the love bestowed and that we are expected to emulate. Considering the ways in which sacrificial love is seen as being at the heart of Christ's mission and surrogacy is projected as the rationale for his violent death, we do not find it hard to believe that God sanctions the surrogate roles black women have performed and are expected to perform, as a servant class to whites and as the presumed property of men. This is certainly the lived reality of many black women, especially those elderly black women I spied at the movies, who undoubtedly had fewer social, political, educational, and employment options than those of my generation and since, yet who sacrificed their time, labor, resources, and aspirations on our behalf.

Sacrifice, however closely related to love, is not the same thing as love. Two important meanings demonstrate how the call to sacrifice can surely result in suffering for love and how it can, as surely, result in the betrayal of the best interests of those called upon to make the sacrifice. Sacrifice means giving up something valued or desirable for the sake of something else having a prior or more important claim, and it involves the conscious, devoted choice and will of those making the sacrifice. This notion of sacrifice is understood as *surrender.* A second meaning is the occasion to allow someone to be injured or put at a disadvantage for the sake of someone else, and it involves the conscious (and unconscious) choices and will of those for whom the sacrifice is made, who are calling upon others to be sacrificed. This idea of sacrifice is *betrayal.*

While not wishing to glorify pain, I do recognize that love and pain are closely bound up together in lived human experience and that my need for a Redeemer is for one who can free me from and *for* the pain of love. I am not a glutton for pain. I have not wanted to risk feeling even love's pain until relatively recently in my life, when I made the choice to become a parent. The imposition of the duty to sacrifice (which can constitute betrayal) does not negate the "is-ness" of sacrifice (as surrender) as an element of love. I know this because of what others who love me surrender on my behalf, relating to me interpersonally and as family, and because of what I am compelled to surrender to them, sometimes gladly, sometimes less so. I sense this is so in my relationship with my God, who loves me and yields to me that grace, forgiveness, challenge, and instruction I need in order to live into my calling as a disciple and a citizen of the world. As a womanist, I hate to admit it, but such surrendering love or *agape* as I am experiencing it—from God, for God, from my daughter, Jada, for her, from others, for others—is *incomprehensible* in its willingness to endure pain when called upon. Thus I believe the Quaker hymnwriter Jennie Evelyn Hussey penned the words to "Lead Me to Calvary" *not* to glorify pain but to signify her desire to surrender completely to the requisites of a living, burning love for someone else, in the manner of Christ Jesus' surrender: "Lest I forget Gethsemane; lest I forget thine agony; lest I forget thy love for me, lead me to Calvary." Hussey spent many years taking care of an invalid sister, in the *imitatio Christi*, in the imitation of Christ, the sovereign of love and of her life and of the lives of those African American women who thanklessly nurture and sustain the black church and community with their time, money, and spirit. Their experiences exemplify perfectly the poignant query of the poet Robert Hayden, "What did I know, what did I know, of love's austere and lonely offices?" and substantiate the claim of my favorite R&B singer, Luther Vandross, that "sometimes love is wonderful but sometimes it's only love." These all raise the question of the relationship between love and justice, what Reinhold Niebuhr calls "mutual love" and feminists and womanists call reciprocity or mutuality, that manner of love I am calling *sacramentality*, that exercise of one's will to love in, with, through, and beyond one's own brokenness.

Atonement and Discipleship

In *The Passion of the Christ*, the memory of both surrendering and mutual love between Jesus and the earliest believers is muted by the film's focus on the brutality of the crucifixion, notwithstanding the flashbacks that showed Jesus counseling the disciples in the manner of love he desired of and for them, despite his heroic rescue of the woman taken in adultery. That he endured so much pain did not come across to me as a sign of his love for us, inciting us to love him back, but as an overbearing message to "the Jews" and the "sinners" among us to relent to the guilt of crucifying him. At the outset, viewers are given the suffering servant passage from Isa. 53:5 to contemplate: "he was wounded for our transgressions, crushed for our iniquities . . . and by his bruises we are healed." I will confess here to my capacity to crucify "again the Son of God" (Heb. 6:6) and admit the possibility that the elderly woman who left the movie in tears *could* have felt implicated in Christ Jesus' suffering, despite my contrary musings. Yet if the substitutionary (read: *surrogacy*) view of the significance of Jesus' suffering and death lifted up here is the only ideological context provided for the violence visited on him, it makes the unrelenting, merciless flogging the more insidious because it suggests that he had to endure an awful lot of suffering to pull it off *pro nobis*—for *all* of us, he endured more than other human beings ever could, and his suffering was more important than that ever endured by other humans.

By disconnecting the death from the very full life that preceded it, we are prevented from contemplating a richer, truer meaning of our salvation and the discipleship that follows from it. We are never prompted to live unto God and for others (doing justice, loving mercy, and walking humbly), as Jesus did, unto death. Instead, we are offered a simplistic salvation by proxy and propitiation, which can never redeem us because we could never merit the sacrifice of any life—human or other animal, much less a god's—nor could we ever be sure if our attempts to appease—presumably, God—are working. In the sixteenth century Martin Luther recognized this in his existential angst, and from his spiritual struggles (*anfechtungen*) was born the substitutionary theory of the Atonement as the foundation for his views on the sacraments he admitted, namely, baptism, penance, and Holy Communion. Protestant theology since has followed Luther in emphasizing the element of surrogacy in Christ Jesus' death as the remedy for sin. However, it has not as closely discerned the distinction between an understanding of the Atonement as penal and propitiatory, that is, as a sacrifice made *in our stead*[16] in an attempt to propitiate or appease God (and turn away God's wrath), and an understanding of the Atonement as remedial and expiatory, that is, as a sacrifice made *on our behalf*[17] that expiates or expunges (much like a court voids a criminal's record) or wipes away sin and guilt and makes communion with ourselves, others, and God possible.

In my own exploration of the moorings of Christian faith, liturgy, and confession, I have found the expiatory, rather than propitiatory, rationale for Christ Jesus' sacrifice to be efficacious for those of us who experience *sin as violation*[18] in our day-to-day lives, who do not merely regard sin as a theological idea but who actually suffer from its alienating, dehumanizing, and self-perpetuating effects. In the light of Hebrew faith and liturgy, Jesus' expiatory sacrifice is the remedy, not merely patchwork relief, for every self- and life-negating impulse I have as a result of the violation that I experience and that I impose on others in my turn. This does not mean that I no longer experience my own sinfulness or vulnerability to the sinfulness of others, but that I can now live with complete assurance of God's love for me forever and with the hope of regeneration that comes with each new day. So, from preexistence to resurrection to intercession, every conceptual element of Christ Jesus' dramatic, life-affirming narrative reckons with the radical reality of sin and violation people experience every day, conveying something of how precious we are to the God who created us and who deigned to die for us and *like us*: "The belief that God, in Christ, shed God's own blood elevates the meaning of the *once for all* nature of Christ Jesus' death. The divine-human dynamic in the story signifies that there is *something* of God in the blood of the cross. . . . It highlights the egregious nature of every historical crime against humanity and the Divinity."[19]

As a people and as individuals, African Americans have understood Christ Jesus' death as a sacramental act endured *for us* out of love and his own volition. As we are mostly Protestants, we simply do not need to espouse notions of the Atonement that do not properly bear witness to the God of our experience in order to spout orthodoxies, Protestant or

Catholic. If in fact we believe the utterance so frequently made in black church settings, "Jesus saved my soul from sin and shame," then why should we continually subject others or ourselves to the re-stigmatizing implications of an Atonement theory that goes only part of the way in addressing the cause and the remedy for the sin that is in us and that is visited upon us? Why not lose the language and spirit of propitiation and embrace that of expiation in our litanies as a sign of our complete faith in a God who loves us and bids us to become God's children? Since God in Christ has bestowed upon us a living, burning love, we might rather explore what that love helps us to become and makes us do and cease lamenting who we are not and what we have done and not done. As I have written elsewhere, "Christians need to ponder the implications of Christ's death continuously, because the drama testifies to the exceedingly great lengths God goes to advise the extent of human estrangement."[20] It also speaks to the infinite, positive possibilities that await us who choose to become, despite what vulnerabilities remain as a consequence of our humanity.

Many Christians today are more scandalized by the humanity than by the presumed divinity of Jesus, and I believe the movie illuminates this by the insane amount of violence his character endures. A real human being would have perished much closer to the beginning of the movie! Even if one believes the twin claims of incarnation that Jesus was fully human and fully divine, it nonetheless does not make him superhuman. That is counterintuitive to the understanding that as God was in Christ, God is in us, yet such an empowerment did not and does not make the conditions of mortal existence less conditioned, less finite, or less vulnerable. It gives us an ethical mandate to deal with each other in truth and love.

More seriously, the bloodless crucifixions that took place next to Jesus in the film are also a scandalous discounting of other human suffering, which I believe is a subtext of the film. But I refuse to believe that Jesus' whipping was more brutal than those of my slave forebears, that his death was more significant or more scandalous than those of six million Jews and five million others who perished in the Holocaust, or of the Japanese people who died in World War II and who are still dying of radiation poisoning,[21] or of the tens of thousands of Americans, Iraqis, Afghans, Nigerians, Indians, Pakistanis, Palestinians, and Israelis who have died in recent violence, or of our mothers and sisters and aunts and friends who have died at the hands of violent people. I refuse to believe his suffering was more real or unremitting than what is visited upon Jews right now because the film makes them a scapegoat. I cannot believe his thorny crown was more painful than even my own existential angst. If one buys the notion that Jesus is Emmanuel, God with us, one misses the point of the story entirely: that God identifies with us in all manner of suffering and does not seek to supersede us in suffering either in quantity or quality, but to persuade us to stop inflicting suffering, once and for all, and to assure us that whatever we suffer, however determined evil is against us, we can and we will be redeemed.

In this present age, evil is insinuated and experienced in a variety of ways in the African American experience. Gone are the days when evil could be discerned in the contorted, gleeful faces of farmers and housewives witnessing a lynching or lobbing stones at innocent school children. The K-9 patrol and the fire hoses, too, once shamelessly used by white authorities to regulate black protestors, have been reassigned to more conventional uses. Although racial and gender violence remain part of the warp and woof of daily life in America, there remain also the results of redlining, unjust distribution of city, county, state, and federal resources (taxation with meager representation), the distortions of "science" to justify white privilege and black oppression, and the disfranchisement of whole segments of populations to guarantee the outcome of elections, to name a few of the ways in which the radical reality of evil makes itself apparent in black life.

Reflecting deeply on the Passion in the African American experience, black and womanist theologians articulate a standard of discipleship that affords others—and especially us—the benefit of a connection to God based on love with justice. Listening to talk radio after the opening of *The Passion of the Christ,* I heard few (if any) black church people make the connections theologians make between their historic and present suffering and that of Christ Jesus. It seems as if they really believe that his Passion, that is, his suffering for love's sake, his own surrender, was more important than any they could ever have experienced or could ever experience, because his very divinity raised the stakes. There is, however, a peculiar office of evil that attempts to render suffering invisible, so that it may go on unopposed in its unholy agendas. When we ignore real suffering, whether it is our own or that of others, or when we despise the tears of those who suffer, as I was tempted to do after viewing the movie, we give to evil an impetus and a substance that it does not merit. We betray our own best interests and others' whom we ignore or despise. And we curtail and deny the divine possibilities vested in our human frame.

For over two millennia now, the life-affirming narrative of Christ Jesus has called upon Christians to exercise our will and right to love ourselves, others, and God. In his whole story, particularly in the *authentic* Passion of the Christ, we are called upon to become the children of God, to be agents of justice who risk brokenness, and to be sacramental witnesses of the steadfast love of God for us—in, with, through, and beyond our brokenness—and to signify our hope of the ultimate victory of love over hatred, justice over oppression, and good over evil, beyond the grave.

4

Identifying with the Cross of Christ

Demetrius K. Williams

Mel Gibson's *The Passion of the Christ*, released on Ash Wednesday, opened to mixed reviews. The element of violence in the depiction of the Passion was a constant theme in several reviews. A. O. Scott of the *New York Times* remarked about the movie that it "is harrowingly violent." He went on to say that Gibson's work "is so relentlessly focused on the savagery of Jesus' final hours that this film seems to arise less from love than from wrath, and to succeed more in assaulting the spirit than in uplifting it. Mr. Gibson has constructed an unnerving and painful spectacle that is also, in the end, a depressing one."[1] Even some reviewers who were favorable toward the movie could not avoid commenting on the violence and vicarious suffering depicted. Lawrence Toppman of the *Charlotte Observer* wrote, "The main message of this drama is driven home with emotional hammer blows: Christ died for your salvation, after enduring more misery than you could ever know. . . . Gibson has made an extraordinary, focused movie with blinders on, showing mostly one color—blood red."[2]

To be sure, Gibson's interpretation of the Passion takes the visual suffering and violence to new and graphic dimensions. However, it is perhaps a historic depiction of the Roman practice of crucifixion, which was a brutal and violent act of the Roman state reserved for criminals and seditionists. As Toppman indicates, the depiction of Jesus' harrowing death forever linked Jesus' Passion and crucifixion to the idea of unmerited redemptive suffering. This idea has had a significant place in Christian theology and church sacraments for centuries; it is the core of the Christian theme of redemption: the teaching that "Christ suffered and died for us (our sins)."

As an African American New Testament scholar and Baptist minister, I have been exposed uncritically to this elemental teaching of the Christian tradition on the values of unmerited suffering within my faith tradition, but with some degree of critical engagement in my academic training. Moreover, as a person who is a part of a historically oppressed community where such ideas have been used to serve the hegemonic goals of the oppressor, I ask: how might this idea be reevaluated? Is there evidence in the New Testament that directs us to a new point of departure? I think so! The Passion, cross, and crucifixion remain important symbols in African American Christian religious traditions as a part of their discourse (preaching and teaching), rituals and liturgy (Lord's Supper, Communion), and worship. Some contemporary black and womanist theologians and scholars are urging African American Christians to do away with, deemphasize, or severely mitigate these foundational symbols. It seems unlikely that they will soon give way to some other symbol because they have had such significance in the Christian tradition in general and the African American tradition in particular.

The Passion in African American Christian Tradition

One might question why the suffering and crucifixion of Jesus has such an appeal to oppressed peoples. In the African American Christian religious tradition, the spirituals are the place to begin for addressing this question because several of them emphasize

identification with Jesus' crucifixion and passion. For many African American Christians the
suffering and death of Jesus spoke in a unique
way to their situation as a community of the
oppressed. Enslaved blacks found it natural to
identify with the sufferings of Jesus because
it was analogous to their own situation. In his
life and example they found a close and intimate ally, which they depicted in the spirituals
as an ever-present and intimate friend:

> He have been wid us, Jesus,
> He still wid us, Jesus
> He will be wid us, Jesus,
> Be wid us to the end.
>
> In de mornin' when I rise,
> Tell my Jesus huddy [howdy] oh;
> I wash my hands in de mornin' glory,
> Tell my Jesus huddy, oh.[3]

Jesus was also the one who "found"
enslaved blacks and helped them to bear their
heavy trials (the cross) and to keep their stability in an unstable world.

> Who found me when I was lost?
> Who helped me to bear my cross?
> Who fixed me up, turned me 'round,
> Left my feet on solid ground?
> I know it was Jesus!
> I know it was my Lord![4]

Since Jesus was their intimate friend and source of stability, it is not surprising that Jesus' suffering (Passion) and cross would appeal to them because they too had been rejected, beaten, and murdered. In Jesus' suffering enslaved blacks saw their own life situation, and with unfettered imagination they described what they felt and saw.[5] With their songs' imaginative descriptions of the Passion, they emphasized a very human Jesus. They described his suffering and pain and imagined themselves present at the crucifixion: "Were you there when they crucified my Lord?"[6] Despite Jesus' pain and suffering, "he never said a mumbling word, he jes hung his head and he died." Another spiritual also finds the black slaves at the foot of the cross. Just as Jesus was present at their side during their trials and suffering, they were also present at Jesus' side.[7]

> They nail my Jesus down
> They put him on the crown of thorns,
> O see my Jesus hanging high!
> He look so pale and bleed so free:
> O don't you think it was a shame,
> He hung there hours and died in dreadful
>   pain?[8]

Jesus died an innocent victim of cruel justice—the same kind of justice that many slaves had experienced. While they were careful to keep their criticisms about their present oppressors in check (or in code!), they did not hold back their judgments about the people who perpetuated such a crime against Jesus. By analogy, they could unleash their sentiments about how white Americans treated them: "The cruel people! They crucified my Lord."[9]

It becomes apparent from some key spirituals on the Passion and death of Jesus that many enslaved blacks believed that Jesus died on the cross for them, and that they had a unique relationship with him. His Passion was a symbol of their suffering and hardships. Undoubtedly they also knew of the agony of rejection and the pain of "hanging on a tree." According to James Cone, "through the experience of being slaves, they encountered the theological significance of Jesus' death: through the crucifixion, Jesus makes an unqualified identification with the poor and the helpless and takes their pain upon himself."[10] Along this same line of thought, they made an insightful comparison: since Jesus did not leave them alone in their oppression, they would also join with him in his suffering. They could imaginatively and ritually, in their singing and worship, join with Jesus in his suffering and he with them because of their

understanding of time: "In the spirituals . . .
a sense of sacred time operated, in which the
present was extended backwards so that characters, scenes, and events from the Old and
New Testaments became dramatically alive
and present."[11] Like them, Jesus suffered and
died the death of a slave (Phil. 2:7), but his
death was meant to put an end to all human
bondage as evidenced by his resurrection and
exaltation (Phil. 2:9-11). This means that the
cross was not the end of God's drama of salvation: there was also vindication.[12]

For some scholars enslaved blacks' views
of the Passion, cross, and crucifixion in the
spirituals bespeaks an ethos that has encouraged slaves and subsequent generations of
blacks to acquiesce to their oppression and
has helped to undermine efforts toward liberation. This same idea about black passivity in
the spirituals, related to their understanding
and identification with the Passion, cross, and
crucifixion, can be seen in a comment made
by Rev. Reverdy Ransom, an African Methodist Episcopal (AME) bishop of the early
twentieth century. He remarked: "Unlike the
American Indian, the Negro did not overthrow
slavery and oppression by violence. They
tried to achieve gentleness of spirit and kindness of heart. The Negro spirituals tell us more
about the hopes and aspirations, the attitude

of mind and the spirit of Negroes than could be learned from volumes of literature on the subject."[13] A similar understanding of the Passion, cross, and crucifixion and approach to addressing the problem of black suffering and liberation can be seen in black moral and religious exhortation. It should not be surprising that the theme of the cross can be found in African American religious instruction and exhortation. This is in keeping with the general tenor of the Christian tradition. Rev. Daniel Alexander Payne, another leading bishop of the AME church in the nineteenth century and founder of Wilberforce University, uses the theme of the cross as the basis of the black Christian's moral and educational fiber:

> Let the education of your children penetrate the heart.—That education which forgets, or purposely omits, the culture of the heart, *is better adapted to devilism than manhood*. But the education which reaches the heart, moulds it, humbles it before the Cross, is rather the work of the homestead than the common school or college. It is given by the *parents* rather than the schoolmaster—by the *mother* rather than the father. . . . But this requires the transforming grace of God; requires that our mothers be women of strong faith and fervent daily prayers; requires that they live beneath the wings of the Cherubim—at the foot of the

Cross—loving the God-man "whose favor
is life, and whose loving kindness is better
than life."[14] [italics in original]

It is interesting to note that for Payne
mothers are the ones to impart the hum-
bling education of the heart modeled on the
cross. Could it be due in part to the passive
and submissive role society and the black
churches have prescribed for women, a role
that enabled women to better reinscribe the
virtues of the Passion, cross, and crucifixion
to their children? This is perhaps the case and
the grounds for the argument that an emphasis on the Passion promotes passivity in black
Christian religious culture in general.

Black preaching has also traditionally
made the proclamation of the Passion, cross,
and crucifixion a central theme. With vivid
imagery and vibrant metaphor, early black
preachers described the crucifixion and its
significance for their black audience. One
nineteenth-century correspondent from Georgia wrote to the editor of the *American Mis-
sionary* that the blacks he had heard speak are
"wonderful preachers!" He then recounted a
sermon of remarkable quality: "The preacher
spoke of the need of atonement for sin. 'Bull-
ocks c'dn't do it, heifers c'dn't do it, de blood
of doves c'dn't do it—but up in heaven, for

thousan and thousan of years, the Son was saying to the Father, "Put up a soul, put up a soul. Prepare me a body, an I will go an meet Justice on Calvary's brow!" I see the sun when she turned herself black. I see the stars a fallin from the sky, and them old Herods comin out of their graves and goin about the city, and they knew 'twas the Lord of Glory.'"[15] Early sermons like this one indicate the importance of the Passion, cross, and crucifixion in the black preaching tradition, which emphasized the fact that Jesus died a horrible death for humanity's sins.

The poet Langston Hughes wrote of the "sorrow songs," the spirituals that he saw encouraging black people to submit to suffering. He made a bold claim regarding the black liberation enterprise: he wrote that Jesus "could not die for me," but instead "only my own hands" would bring him freedom.[16] Hughes as a representative of the "New Negro," intellectually astute and wise to the ways of the world, found the black Christian identification with and hope in Jesus, not to mention the positive suffering encouraged by the Passion, inadequate to address the problem of black oppression. Indeed, even to look to God or Jesus is a part of bygone days. For him, and some others within the black experience in America, a rejection of God and

religion and an embracing of human efforts
alone are the means of liberation. Hughes is
implicitly drawing upon an overlooked perspective in the African American experience,
black humanism.

Anthony B. Pinn has recently explored the
black humanistic tradition and the question
of evil and suffering in the black experience
in America in his book *Why Lord?* His primary argument with the African American
Christian religious experience is the notion of
redemptive suffering, which black Christianity
actually inherited from the early Christian tradition. "Positive suffering maintains the possibility of divinely sanctioned oppression. It is
because of this possibility that any religious
explanation for suffering that hints at redemptive suffering should be avoided . . . [because]
it lessens a sense of accountability and responsibility on the part of oppressors. . . . And for
the oppressed, it blurs a proper understanding
of suffering as demonic, thereby significantly
softening the perception of suffering as irre-
ducibly and existentially damaging. In short,
movement toward liberation should involve a
desire for change brought about by a proper
understanding of suffering as unquestionably
and unredeemably evil."[17] Pinn observes further that the problem of suffering and evil has
been resolved in three ways in the Christian

religious tradition: (1) to rethink the nature of evil and suffering, (2) to rethink the power of God (wherein humans become God's co-workers), and (3) to question God's goodness/righteousness (better known as "theodicy"). A fourth way that Pinn suggests, a "questioning/denial of God's existence," which he offers as a "religious" option, *is not* an option for most African American Christians.[18] At any rate, his critique and proposal are directed primarily to the discipline of black theology, not to the church.

Womanist scholars and theologians, on the other hand, have critiqued the way in which the Passion, cross, and crucifixion have functioned within African American Christian communities. The traditional understanding and interpretation of the Passion have been used, it is argued, to valorize sacrifice by sacralizing violence upon the oppressed and promoting surrogacy among black women. For this reason Delores S. Williams writes, regarding the symbols of Christ's crucifixion and death:

> Should these images, infused with pre-meditated violence, maintain their status as major sacred emblems of our faith? Or are there other images from the story of Jesus that can better reflect those elements Christians in future generations should remem-

ber about the story—images that suggest the justice, peace, and healing so prominent in many of our narratives about Jesus? . . . It matters not that these images are meant to communicate something about the salvation brought to humankind. . . . The reality is that, at some level, the cross is a constant reminder of innocent suffering and violence, regardless of the message it is supposed to communicate about salvation. Too often, Christians are thereby taught to believe that something good can result from violence.[19]

In response to such trends, Williams offers the ministry and resurrection of Jesus as focal points for a more liberative alternative for oppressed peoples in order to counter the high redemptive value the Christian religion puts on suffering.[20] Christian theology and iconography focused on the Passion serve as constant reminders of this value placed on Jesus' death. Since, for Williams, Jesus' crucifixion remains a violent act of murder and every time a cross or crucifix is seen, we are reminded of this murder, "perhaps our concern should be to emphasize not what Jesus died for but what he lived for—mercy, justice, healing, and spiritual transformation of humankind."[21] Her concern is a matter of proper focus because she does not propose a total rejection of the cross and crucifixion. She does think that there are some compelling reasons for remembering them. Both represent symbols of realism that remind us of "what can happen to reformers who successfully challenge the status quo and try to bring about a new dispensation of love and power for the poor. For those who really try to live out the two sole commandments Jesus left us—to love God with all our heart, soul, and mind, and to love our neighbor as ourselves—the cross and crucifixion remind us of the struggle that lies ahead."[22]

The Passion, cross, and crucifixion have had some "toxic" effects in the African American religious experience by promoting the idea of redemptive suffering (Pinn) and the acceptance of innocent suffering and violence (Williams). But these symbols and their accompanying meanings will not be easily disregarded in the Christian tradition in general or the black Christian tradition in particular. As Amos Jones writes, "The black church must continue to combat the surging theological forces that militate against it by stringently adhering to the crucifixion and resurrection of Jesus Christ. . . . The crucifixion and resurrection . . . [have] been the dynamic force and unifying power of the black church since American slavery."[23] My approach then is not to disregard the Passion, cross, and crucifixion because of their negative effects, but to reinterpret them using an overlooked tradition, biblical-critical interpretation. Paul's early formulation and articulation of the cross as a polemical metaphor and as the basis for God's new eschatological community, which is engaged in a struggle to constitute and maintain its identity in the Greco-Roman world, offer new insight into the current debate in African American and general theological discourse. In this regard, Paul's rhetorical articulations employing crucifixion terminology are not intended to promote or encourage suffering or violence, but to struggle against the forces that seek to fragment or mitigate human community and integrity.

The Cross and Crucifixion in Pauline Rhetoric

It is difficult to exaggerate the importance of the Passion, cross, and crucifixion of Jesus Christ for Paul—it energized his entire apostolic endeavor.[24] What New Testament scholars and the Christian tradition have not clearly distinguished is Paul's theology of the death of Jesus from his rhetorical terminology of the cross. Paul inherited a theology of the death of Jesus from the early Christian tradition. The terms such as *blood* (*heima*) and *expiation* (*hilasterion*) and the phrases "for us" and "on our behalf" represent received language from the early Christian tradition.[25] Such terms and language are borrowed from the Jewish sacrificial cult, wherein animals are sacrificed (their blood is shed) "on behalf of" and to atone (expiate) for human sinfulness. Paul uses this language in his letters, to be sure, but I suggest that this is the kind of language that he uses to build his theology of the death of Jesus.[26]

Paul's terminology (such as *cross* and *crucifixion*) is not used as a foundation for his theology of Jesus' death as such but for his rhetorical challenges and struggles to maintain the integrity of the early church community.[27] The terminology of the cross (which Paul calls his *logos tou staurou*, "discourse/message of the cross" in 1 Cor. 1:18) is Paul's "fighting" (polemical) language. For this reason, it is found almost exclusively (except for Rom. 6:6) in polemical contexts (see 1 Corinthians 1–4; 2 Corinthians 10–13; Gal. 2:19; Phil. 2:8; 3:18).

Paul's cross terminology is never directly related to suffering. According to J. C. Beker, Paul never sanctifies or hallows death, pain, and suffering. There is no hint of masochistic delight in suffering and death. Beker argues further that a theology of the cross (I prefer "discourse of the cross" to underscore its rhetorical nature) must be distinguished from a theology of the death and resurrection of Jesus and of the suffering of Jesus.[28] This is an important starting point for a new perspective on the Passion, cross, and crucifixion for the African American religious tradition. I suggest that other early interpreters conflated the rhetorical aspects of the crucifixion, which Paul used in his contestations with his opponents and as a metaphor and basis for communal identity and struggle, with the language and imagery of the Passion (suffering). Paul's terminology was his own contribution to the theology of the early church: he used it as a provocative symbol that could unite Jew and Gentile and serve as the basis for an inclusive vision of human community. As such, Paul's discourse of the cross challenged and countered the social-religious prerogatives of both Jewish (Philippians 3 and Galatians) and Gentile (1 Corinthians 1–4; 2 Corinthians 10–13) society. Some New Testament scholars (the present writer included) have begun to unearth the political function and nature of Paul's cross terminology: the cross and crucifixion, seen on the broader canvas of Greco-Roman imperial society and culture, can be viewed as *anti-imperial*.[29] Thus crucifixion terminology, as a rhetorical or argumentative metaphor, could be used by Paul to express a wide range of theological, ethical, social, ecclesial, and *political* concerns, but not to promote suffering and passivity! Passion imagery and language must be understood as separate in intention from crucifixion terminology.

The terminology of the cross and crucifixion serves as an important metaphor in 1 Corinthians for articulating the nature and content of the Christian community, a new Israel composed of both Jews and Gentiles. Paul's use of this terminology for community building is expressed vividly in 1 Cor. 1:22-24: "For Jews demand signs and Greeks desire wisdom, but we proclaim Christ crucified, a stumbling block to Jews and foolishness to Gentiles, but to those who are the called, both Jews and Greeks, Christ the power of God and the wisdom of God." The polemical edge is evident in Paul's realization that the cross is offensive in both Jewish and Greco-Roman culture. In addition, the element of community building is present in his statement that "to the called," which referred to members of the new eschatological community of believers, Christ is the power and wisdom of God. So here in the crucifixion of Christ Paul finds the rhetorical basis to construct a new community that is diametrically opposed to both Jewish and Gentile cultural and religious prerogatives and Greco-Roman social and cultural values.

The sociopolitical nature of Paul's cross terminology can be discerned in his declaration that the cross is the "power of God." Through the proclamation of the cross the *power* of God is revealed—a power that creates a new community, "the called," composed of both Jew and Greek (Gentile) (1 Cor. 1:24). The cross is a "stumbling block to Jews" and "foolishness to Gentiles," but to those who are "the called" it is the power and wisdom of God: it represents God's creative power to bring into existence a new people whose praxis and social vision are counter to worldly wisdom and standards (1 Cor. 2:1-13). The reality is that crucifixion was a cruel and violent act of Roman power and hegemony. But through Jesus Christ's resurrection it was transformed into a new political-religious symbol, a symbol whose sovereign is not Caesar but Christ. Through the proclamation of the cross God was establishing an alternative society to that of Rome.[30] Viewing crucifixion terminology in 1 Corinthians from this perspective exposes its political edge. Paul's cross terminology in 1 Corinthians then represents a struggle to maintain communal identity against the evil and destructive forces of Roman imperial cultural values and society.

In Philippians 2 Paul employs cross terminology again to encourage communal unity

(2:1-4, 8), using the story of Christ as a paradigmatic example. Christ in this narrative
(2:5-11) serves as an example of faithfulness
to God and to others-in-community in the
struggle against the forces of evil and bondage. Christ identifies with the slave (2:7) in
this passage, which is considered the lowest
status in Greco-Roman society, to show the
depths to which he would descend to bring
freedom and wholeness to the least of all. As
in 1 Corinthians, Philippians 3 also engages
religious and sociopolitical realities. Paul
attempts to counter the socioreligious claims
of his Jewish-Christian opponents that they
represent the "true" circumcision and heritage
of Israel (Phil. 3:2) by stating that those who
are "in Christ" are the "true" circumcision
(Phil. 3:3-4). The Jewish-Christian missionaries were attempting to convince the young
Philippian community to adopt the Jewish
identity symbol of circumcision in order to
avoid or mitigate persecution (cf. 1 Cor. 1:27-
30; 3:2). For Paul this counters the emphasis
of the cross/crucifixion, which entails loyalty
to Christ and the maintenance of the vision
and integrity of community even in the face
of persecution. The political edge is evident
in this passage in Paul's use of the term *polit-
euma* in 3:20, which translates as "common-
wealth" or even "citizenship," and in 1:27

with the related term *politesthai* ("live as citizens"). Those who encourage the Philippian church to forsake the cross-founded community for a "legal" status within Judaism and protected by Roman sociopolitical policy are considered as "enemies of the cross of Christ" (3:18) because they have founded their version of Christianity on circumcision and seek social and political security from Rome, not from Christ. In Paul's estimation the Philippians and all those "in Christ" realize that the cross is the foundation of a new religious, social, and, by virtue of being an alternative society, political reality. Their citizenship and loyalty are not to the Roman emperor or his civil-religious cult, but to Jesus Christ who is their Savior (*soter*, 3:20). He will, in due time, transform all things. The communal and sociopolitical nature of Paul's cross terminology should not be overlooked in Philippians.

Finally, in Galatians Paul's crucifixion terminology supplies the basis for his discourse on the freedom of the Christian from the Law and circumcision. Paul's discourse of the cross in Galatians indicates his struggle to maintain the integrity of the Christian community against the denial of Gentile freedom and the unity of Jew and Gentile. Indeed, the crucifixion of Christ is the basis upon which he builds his notion of justification (2:14-21).

Paul argues that as a result of the proclamation of the crucified Christ (3:1), Gentiles have received the promise of the Spirit (3:2-5), and their present existence as the people of God is a fulfillment of the promise to Abraham (3:6-18). Since the promise of Abraham is prior to the Law, the Law had only limited effect (3:19-22). Now that faith has been wrought (through the crucifixion of Christ), all who are baptized in Christ are one (Gal 3:27-28). The barriers of race ("Jew nor Greek"), class ("slave nor free"), and gender ("male and female") have been overcome through the cross. This is the ultimate result of the cross for Paul: it unites a divided humanity. The importance of the cross and crucifixion in Paul's rhetoric should not be underestimated:

> As soon as we recognize the centrality of the cross of Christ for Paul, the common view that Paul is uninterested in political realities should leave us perplexed. The crucifixion of Jesus is, after all, one of the most unequivocally political events recorded in the New Testament. Behind the early theological interpretations of Jesus' crucifixion as a death 'for us' and behind centuries of piety that have encrusted the crucifixion with often grotesque sentimentality, stands the 'most nonreligious and horrendous feature of the gospel,' the brutal fact of the cross as an instrument of imperial terror.[31]

Paul's crucifixion terminology has therefore
not obscured the nature of the cross as historical and political oppression. According to
Neil Elliot, "only a gentile church unaccus-
tomed to that perspective, and more familiar
with the sacrificial logic of the blood cults,
could have transformed Paul's message into
a cult of atonement in Christ's blood (the letter to the Hebrews) and a charter of Israel's
disfranchisement (the *Letter of Barnabas*)."[32]
In the beginning it was not so. It is possible
in contemporary terms to suggest then that
"Paul's doctrine of the cross is thus a doctrine
of God's justice and God's partiality toward
the oppressed."[33]

So there is a way of maintaining the symbol and concept of the cross/crucifixion that
does not entail redemptive suffering, violence,
or the hallowing of death. It can serve as a
social-political and religious-communal symbol that supplies a basis for corporate identity
and the discursive ammunition for struggle
and resistance.

The Cross as Symbol of Unity
in Struggle

Although the original intention of crucifixion
terminology in Paul's proclamation was not
intended to glorify or hallow suffering and

passivity, the symbol and concept of the cross were transformed and used in America as an ideological tool of oppression. The Passion, cross, and crucifixion, used as symbols of innocent (and redemptive) suffering and the acceptance of humility, served the hegemonic goals of the slave regime and segregationists. The "white" cross that burned in the front lawns of victimized blacks was used as a symbol of white violence, control, and brutality. Hence, the cross and the passive acceptance of suffering are viewed as inseparable companions. This was not the original intention of Paul's cross terminology: on the contrary, he attempted to promote a more inclusive and united humanity, using the language of struggle against the forces of fragmentation and evil. Recently womanists and black theologians have argued that Paul's theology of the cross is no longer valid for the self-understanding and liberation goals of African American churches because it encourages passivity and can exonerate the oppressor's violence against the weak. My contention is that a renewed understanding of the cross will not validate vicarious suffering or acceptance of oppression. Instead, the metaphor of the cross has served as a symbol of communal struggle for African American religious communities, particularly in the African American

liberation and protest tradition that sought to
struggle for an inclusive view of human community. Thus the metaphor of the crucifixion is compatible with the African American
tradition of protest against racism and other
forms of oppression.

In this regard, it is important to realize that
African Americans, as well as others who are
victims of oppression, have two basic options
available to them when the balance of power
(that is, wealth, weapons, and institutions) is
not in their favor: (1) accept the oppressor's
value system and acquiesce to their allotted
social station or (2) find other resources (that
is, religious, social, legal, and discursive) that
enable them to fight against oppression. The
African American Christian religious tradition
chose the latter, using Jesus Christ and the
Bible as the bedrock of their struggle.[34] Since
symbols are important in human societies
because they "point to dimensions of reality
that cannot be spoken of literally,"[35] African
Americans chose in several cases the symbol
of the cross, not only because it represented
dimensions of their own situation of oppression, but also because they could join with
Christ in the struggle for liberation.[36] As far
as they were concerned, Jesus died *and rose*
so that blacks and others who are oppressed
might struggle for liberation. Faith in Jesus

Christ did not necessarily lead all blacks to passivity. I concur with James Cone that "the idea that Jesus make blacks passive is simply a misreading of the black religious experience."[37] Human suffering that emerges from active engagement to challenge political, social, and religious injustices aligns itself with Jesus' struggle for human liberation. In the African American Christian religious tradition many blacks viewed their allegiance to the cross not as a passive endurance of slavery and racism (or sexism for that matter), but rather as a means of arguing for freedom and equity.

In the battle against slavery and racism, one ex-slave expressed the significance of Jesus' death for blacks by claiming "that he learned from his mother and father the potentially revolutionary doctrine 'that God is no respecter of persons, but gave his son to die for all, bond or free, black or white, rich or poor,' and that 'God protects those whom he chooses to sanctify for some task.'"[38] This "potentially revolutionary doctrine" that he learned from his parents combined several elements of the African American protest tradition: Acts 10:34 ("God is no respecter of persons"), an allusion to Gal. 3:28, and the significance of Christ's death for human unity and equality. Both passages of scripture and the important reference to Jesus' death are a part of the essential arsenal of biblical passages that supported blacks' arguments for freedom and equality.

For many black women the call to freedom and equality within American society should also have entailed equality within the church. Jarena Lee, a black woman preacher of the nineteenth century, came to Richard Allen, the founder of the AME church, to seek validation for her call to preach. (Such validation was not immediately forthcoming.) She applied the teaching of Jesus' "death for all" as the foundation for equality within the black church. Lee said, "O how careful we ought to be, lest through our bylaws of church government and discipline, we bring into disrepute even the word of life. . . . Why should it be thought impossible, heterodox, or improper, for a woman to preach? *Seeing that the Savior died* for the woman as well as the man."[39] Her statement underscores the importance of Jesus' death in arguments for freedom and equality in church and society.

Bishop Reverdy Ransom, considered in his time to be a "race man," one who advocated for black people, was intensely engaged in the struggle for black freedom and equality. In several of his sermons and speeches, he employs many of the passages and classic arguments for black equality (for example, Acts 2; 10:34; 17:26; Gal. 3:28). Ransom argued that the cross of Christ, understood correctly, should render invalid any and all arguments for black oppression.

> I have said America is God's proving ground for the Negro. Yea, more, is it not our proving ground for God? The Negro, the last untried human reserve God has at his command, was suddenly thrust from his native jungle and forest and delivered fettered and chained into the severest test that has ever been applied to the teachings of Jesus since Christ was lifted up on the cross. . . . [But] God has declared He can take the "things that are weak to confound the mighty." He says He can take the "Things that are and make them as though they were not." May we not look here for love among all brothers to prove and vindicate the all-fatherhood of God? Shall the Negro live to voice the cry, "There is no God in the affairs of men"? Or shall he and the white man in America prove the cross of Christ superior to differences of color and race?[40]

For Ransom the cross of Christ should have practical social and political results in a Christian nation—including the elimination of racism. Ransom's argument relied on passages used over and again in African American pro-

test discourse and language (in this case Acts
2 and 17:26). He viewed Jesus' struggle in
Roman Judea as analogous to the American
situation: "Jesus Christ founded Christianity
in the midst of the most bitter and intense
antagonisms of race and class. Yet he ignored
them all, dealing alike with Jew, Samaritan,
Syro-Phoenician, Greek and Roman." Ransom
named race and class as the two social challenges of Jesus' ministry that were eradicated
by the crucifixion: "The crowning object at
which Jesus Christ aimed was, 'to break down
the middle wall of partition,' between man and
man, and to take away all the Old Testament
laws and ordinances that prevented Jew and
Gentile from approaching God on an equal
plane. And this He did, 'that He might recon-
cile both unto God in one body by the cross,
having slain the enmity thereby, so making
peace.' [Ephesians 2:14-15]."[41] Ransom quoted
Ephesians, one of Paul's earliest interpreters,
to underscore the significance of the cross for
the early Pauline churches. Like his teacher
Paul, Ransom understood the cross as a vehicle that unifies Jew and Gentile.

Ozro T. Jones, a bishop in the Church of
God in Christ (COGIC), views the death of
Jesus as eliminating the barriers of race, class,
and sex and creating an equality that opens
the doors of freedom for all people. He states:

"*For persons for whom Christ died* any incidental physical condition is no longer a barrier to freedom, or dignity, or value as a person whether that physical condition be social distinction, be race ('Jew or Greek'), class ('bond or free'), or sex ('male or female'). They all share one spiritual destiny and nature and value in Christ. They all are 'fellow heirs' of the promise in Christ" (emphasis in the original).[42] Jones has touched upon the significance of the crucifixion as articulated in Gal. 3:28, the final result of which is the breakdown of the traditional barriers to human freedom, unity, and equality. For Jones this was accomplished through the death of Christ.

My final examples of crucifixion terminology come from the socioreligious ministry of Martin Luther King Jr. While many have critiqued King's notion of redemptive suffering, his notion of the crucifixion did not lead him to passivity but direct and active protest against the forces of injustice. King claimed that directly challenging American racism and economic injustice "is the cross that we must bear for the freedom of our people."[43] For King, to be a Christian is to engage in struggle: "The cross we bear precedes the crown we wear. To be a Christian one must take up his cross, with all of its difficulties and agonizing and tension-packed content and carry it until that very cross leaves its marks upon us and redeem us to that more excellent way which comes only through suffering."[44] While a view of suffering as redemptive could be read here, King clearly believed in the cross as a symbol of struggle against oppression.

King's use of cross terminology moved from the realm of oral suasion to a motivating force for social change. King expressed this idea further in his speech "Suffering and Faith": "There are some who still find the cross a stumbling block, and others consider it foolishness, but I am more convinced than ever before that is the power of God unto social and personal individual salvation. So like the Apostle Paul I can now humbly yet proudly say, 'I bear in my body the marks of the Lord Jesus.'"[45] Reflecting upon Paul's discussion of the cross in 1 Cor. 1:17-25, King understood it to be the power of God for personal and *social* salvation. This move from viewing the cross as the means of purely individual salvation to the addition of the social is a particular emphasis and contribution of African American socioreligious protest. This is similar to Paul's understanding of the cross: the power of God to bring about a new community founded upon a vision of human unity. The achievement of the social vision of human unity and dignity in a world fraught with injustice and oppression means that one might be labeled an extremist. Like Ransom, who viewed blacks' challenge of racism and classism as analogous to Jesus' own ministry, King understood the criticism of himself as an extremist as akin to what Jesus attempted to do in his ministry—establish justice and equity, which ultimately resulted in Christ's crucifixion. Extremism is what characterizes those who fight for social justice and social change:

> So the question is not whether we will be extremist but what kind of extremist will we be? Will we be extremist for hate or will we be extremist for love? Will we be extremist for the preservation of injustice—or will we be extremist for the cause of justice? In that dramatic scene on Calvary's hill, three men were crucified. We must not forget that all three were crucified for the same crime—the crime of extremism. Two were extremist for immorality, and thusly fell below their environment. The other, Jesus Christ, was an extremist for love, truth and goodness, and thereby rose above his environment. So, after all, maybe the South, the nation and the world are in dire need of creative extremists.[46]

To be sure, the world is indeed in need of such extremism for justice. King could remain hopeful about change, even in the face of racist evils and violence perpetuated against black people, because in the crucifixion and resurrection of Jesus he could see the ultimate triumph of good over evil, justice over injustice. "Evil may so shape events," he said, "that Caesar will occupy a palace and Christ a cross, but one day that same Christ will rise up and split history into A.D. and B.C., so that even the life of Caesar must be dated by his name."[47] King also realized that one who is an extremist for justice might lose his or her life in the struggle: "When I took up the cross, I recognized its meaning. . . . The cross is something that you bear, and ultimately that you die on."[48]

The Cross and African American Liberation

Crucifixion terminology viewed as separate from Passion language and imagery exposes it as a powerful metaphor for the active engagement against the forces of social evil and injustice. Such an understanding of the cross and crucifixion has its roots in Pauline rhetoric and the black Christian protest tradition. For this reason, it has been a central component to the African American struggle for liberation and will most likely remain as such, as JoAnne Terrell has asserted: "Perhaps the cross is central to black Christian identity because black Christians suffer, like Jesus and the martyrs, unjustly. . . . I do not think that the problem is with the imagery per se; the cross, in its original sense, embodied a *scandal*, that something, anything, good could come out of such an event. Seen in this light, Jesus' sacrificial act was not the objective. Rather, it was the tragic, if foreseeable, result of his confrontation with evil. This bespeaks a view of Jesus and the martyrs as empowered, *sacramental*, witnesses, not as victims who passively acquiesced to evil."[49] The crucifixion as a symbol may be interpreted by some as validating passive suffering, but in the African American Christian tradition it has more often stood for an inclusive vision of human community and a powerful image of struggle against oppression and for liberation.

5.

Womanist Passion

Karen Baker-Fletcher

Trees

Girls
Dressed in brown,
dance, bend
dance, wind
dance, curve...
green leaves
dance, twining
 arms, branching
falling, weeping,
rising, reaching,
hands and feet
stained . . .
blood on
leaves and
blood on
roots . . .

trees
that weep . . .
trees
that protest
desecration
of earth,
 flesh,
sap,
wounded green
 blood,
dancing
memory
of
breath . . .
re-member-ing
Children . . .

                    —Karen Baker-Fletcher

The above verses are revised excerpts of a poem written in response to a Christian liturgical choreo-poem created by Vanessa Baker and Cheryl Swann for St. Luke "Community" United Methodist Church in Dallas. The longer poem is available in my book *Loves the Spirit: A Womanist Relational Dance of the Trinity.*[1] Baker and Swann's choreo-poem was performed during African American History Month, February 9, 2002, to commemorate the lament and the resurrection hope of Mamie Till Bradley Mobley, the mother of Emmett Till. Till was the fourteen-year-old victim of a 1955 hate crime by white racial supremacists who hated black Americans. He was beaten, disfigured, and lynched, and then his body was thrown into the Mississippi river to hide the crime. From the late nineteenth century until the mid twentieth century many black men, as well as some women and children, were killed in this way by racial supremacists in the United States, especially, but not exclusively, in the South. When the bodies were hung on trees, blood fell onto the leaves, branches, and roots, giving them the appearance of weeping with the dead.

In the performance of Baker and Swann's poem about Emmett Till's lynching and his mother's lament, a teenage boy played the part of Emmett Till. A mature woman played Emmett Till's mother. Billie Holliday's song "Strange Fruit," whose lyrics were written by a Jewish man, played in the background. Teenage girls played the parts of poplar trees with blood at the leaves and blood at the root. The players in the choreo-poem represented intergenerational black communal experience of the ongoing existence of crucifixion, crimes of hatred against those who offer any appearance of stepping out of one's place in relation to emperors, Caesars—representations of worldly, oppressive powers, be they white racial supremacists or economic forces that rob the poor.

I am a womanist theologian and a process theologian. The African American novelist Alice Walker introduced the term *womanist* in 1983.[2] The term *womanist* is derived from the black folk expression "You're acting woman-ish," as in "grown up and in charge." A wom-anist is audacious and courageous.[3] Courage is the embodied power of the Spirit to make or find a way out of no way, to be delivered from evil, and to set the captives free. The terms *womanist* and *womanish* are whole, singular words that signify the wholeness of what it means to be a black woman who resists gender, racial, sexual, and class oppression. They need no qualifier before or after them, demanding that African Americans decide which they are first: black or female and, accordingly, whose liberation comes first. *Womanist* is a holistic term that signifies holistic healing and free-dom of entire communities.

Black women have had to learn to love themselves and others, regardless of what dominant worldly authorities claim, in the power of the Spirit. There is something over-whelmingly powerful—something more than mere flesh and blood, undoubtedly the very energy that creates flesh and blood—that makes love in the midst of hate crimes possible. In the experience of existential evil the temptation to hate in kind, along with the temptations to give into bitterness, passivity, or nihilism, is ever present. A power greater than flesh alone makes it possible to choose love instead—something greater and more persuasive than the urges to seek revenge. Otherwise, more white men would have hung from trees in revenge, because more black women would have encouraged sons, husbands, lovers, brothers, uncles, and fathers to retaliate in kind. Instead, the predominant cultural and spiritual lesson in black culture has been to resist the temptation to hate.

This does not mean that the lesson has been learned perfectly. Uncertainty about what it means to walk in love with power, when the lesson of love has been incompletely taught or learned, has often resulted in internalized hatred and violence against self and one another. Yet wisdom, more fully tapped by some at some times than by others in other times, is available. The wisest of black communities have drawn from the sagacious power of the Spirit to create beauty out of ugliness, celebrate life in the midst of suffering, and walk in love in the midst of hate. Womanists attribute this power to love to the Spirit.

This womanist relational Christology draws on process metaphysics, Christian literature, and, both constructively and critically, writings by Alice Walker. It articulates the distinctive experiences of women of color who lament the violent loss and rape of loved ones because of the color of their skin or because they are black and also women. Process theology is a form of relational theology that emphasizes the integration between spirit and matter, body and Spirit, God and the world.

In process thought, not only do we humans experience God, but God *prehends* or experiences the world, responding to its praise, joy, laments, and suffering. In black women's Christian experience the Holy Spirit, known through Jesus the Christ, experiences the world. It is present in the moanings, groanings, and utterances of the believer who prays for self and world. Again, God, in the power of the Holy Spirit, knows our needs and our hearts, because God intimately experiences and responds to the pain and joy of God's creation. This is what is meant by "prehension." It is God's feeling or concrete, experiential knowledge of creation. Likewise, we experience or prehend God, responding to the call of God positively or negatively. What makes God different is that God knows the world, all of creation, in whole, while we know God and the rest of creation only in part. In black Christian culture, there is an expression about the experience of God: "When you know that you know that you know!" No one can persuade many black Christians that God does not exist or that Jesus is not real, because they have an internal, experiential knowing. Process metaphysics is perhaps the only Western metaphysics that values such claims to internal knowing of the divine. Knowing God is a positive prehension, a feeling of feeling, of God's initial aim for the well-being of self and all of creation. The experiences of racial and sexual hate crimes are negative prehensions, which are overcome by the creative, loving power and call of the divine.

Black women and other women of color experience and mourn hate crimes, racial and sexual. Black women globally ask, "Who is God for us? What is God experiencing in the midst of evil and suffering, and how can we know that God is actually with us, present to help us survive and overcome it?" In 1998 James Byrd was brutally beaten, chained, and then dragged, ultimately decapitated, by three white supremacists driving a pickup truck. James Byrd's mother did not become bitter but, like Emmett Till's mother and like Mary, the mother of Jesus, acted in the belief that love overcomes evil. This "unsurpassable love," to use the words of Charles Hartshorne,[4] protests the injustice of racial hatred and seeks the salvation, which means healing and wholeness, of one's adversaries as well as healing and wholeness for self, family, and community. It works toward right relationship in the universe so that all might experience the love of divine justice. This unsurpassable love is, to use the words of Anna Julia Cooper, "an irresistible power not ourselves."[5]

In the power of the Spirit, black women have found love that overcomes suffering, violence, and injustice: it manifests as nonviolent resistance to injustice; it is not passive, but active. In the life of Martin Luther King Jr. it manifested as nonviolent, direct action. Ella Baker, an older civil rights leader, helped young African American students organize the Student Nonviolent Coordinating Committee. These students participated in nonviolent direct action grounded in love for one's friends and for one's enemies. Coretta Scott King, King's widow, profoundly embodies the forgiveness and resistance of this love while actively demanding justice. This love persuasively resists evil while desiring the well-being of all.

John Cobb and David Griffin have been sufficiently influenced by the power of this persuasive love to discern a truth that many African Americans, male and female, have also acknowledged. Namely, these process metaphysicians observe that this type of creative, persuasive, unsurpassable, passionate, and compassionate love is the power that makes liberation possible.[6] Both King and Howard Thurman were familiar with the metaphysics inspired by the ideas of Alfred North Whitehead, particularly through the writing of Henry Nelson Wieman. It is no surprise, then, that process philosophical understandings of the power of persuasive love in the universe has commonalities with African American theological praxis.[7] This is no sentimental, weak love, but love that has power. A womanist process Christology emphasizes what Hartshorne calls "unsurpassable," "cosmic love."[8] This love is God's action toward the world: God is love. Alfred North Whitehead places this love in the fourth creative phase, "in which the universe accomplishes its actuality." In this final creative phase, "the love of God for the world," an eschatological consummation occurs. Specifically, heaven and the world are integrated, so that the initial aim of God is realized on earth as in heaven.[9]

In process metaphysics, reality is made up of events or "drops of experience." We as individuals are drops of experience. We are an event or, more precisely, a succession of events in a dynamic process of becoming. This is another way of saying that we are not quite the same person we were a moment ago or fifteen years ago. We are each a society made up of cell energy, fueled by the power of creativity itself. As individuals we also participate in divine creativity by creating what we most often think of as societies in everyday life: black churches, communities, families, nations. Just as the cells of our bodies are interrelated and interdependent, so are we human beings interrelated and interdependent with one another. When we are not in right relationship, we meet with destruction. While perishing is a natural part of life—shedding old cells to develop new healthy ones—violent destruction is a problem of evil. When our relationships are not loving, there is unnecessary loss of life—physical, mental, emotional, and spiritual. Followers of Jesus pray for just loving relationships because, according to the teachings of Jesus, the greatest commandments are to love God and neighbor (Luke 10:25-37).

Think of the commandment to pray without ceasing. Christians pray because Christians believe prayer changes things. To pray without ceasing is to desire the well-being of one's becoming in relation to the becoming of others in a dynamic universe. God is continuously re-creating the universe, including the hearts, minds, and bodies of each entity.

It is for this renewal of life and heart that we pray. To desire the well-being of others is to participate in divine love. Each individual is a society, made up of dynamically moving cells and subquantum particles of energy, whether a rock, a tree, a leaf, a sparrow, or a human being whose every hair has been given life by the Spirit.[10] In each moment the old self perishes, and God creates us anew to the extent we do not choose self-destruction in God's creative stead. If God creates anew in each moment, then there is hope for renewed hearts and minds, more just, righteous love in the universe. We pray without ceasing because there is hope for positive transformation in God.

God, who is Spirit, lovingly apprehends every hair of a person's head or every faltering flap of a baby sparrow's wings. This love of God, who is Spirit, is fully manifest, Christians believe, in the life and teachings of Jesus. Christians understand Jesus according to the New Testament accounts of the apostles, who experienced Jesus as *Christ*, meaning "the anointed one" of God—the divine power the apostles, widows, orphans, and many crowds experienced in Jesus. While it is available to all of humanity and to all creatures, it takes on novel meaning in the lives of African American women.

The Spirit in Womanist Thought

For womanists, the Spirit is in creation. In this womanist process Christology the Spirit is the power that brings life out of death. This is possible because Spirit, the power of life, is omnipresent, intimately related to the world and the many bodies in it, in and beyond time. Indeed, Whitehead writes that the world is God's body. God has created it, is creating it, and will continue to recreate this cosmological body, containing many bodies, that has emerged from seeming nothingness. If God is omnipresent in the universe, then there is, as the psalmist writes, no place where God is not. The longed for, consummate integration of heaven and earth is present and yet to come in the saving love that permeates the universe. There is hope for all creation. If the power of life is omnipresent and if it can inspire love of the hater regardless of the temptation to hate the hater, then it is all-inclusive love: it is more powerful than the temptation to hate, loving even the hater, persuasively luring, to use Whitehead's term, or calling, to use the church language of the folk, all into right relationship.

Such love neither fears nor gives in to oppression. To the contrary, it overcomes fear and resists oppression. Cobb and Griffin are

not the first to observe that liberation movements require an understanding of God as
responsive to the world, as loving and continuously creating.[11] For several centuries,
black mothers have taught this wisdom to
sons and daughters encountering the violence
of hatred for the first time. Divine, loving,
creative activity is the power of liberation
movement. Without cosmic, creating love the
world is bereft of hope for redemption and
deliverance. This unsurpassable, cosmic love
unites God and the world in an ongoing, con-
summating process to fully realize the reign
of God.

Anna Julia Cooper was a black feminist
Christian educator; she was born in 1858 and
was an educator in Washington, D.C., until she
retired at the age of ninety.[12] Cooper described
God as "an irresistible power not ourselves"
and as "a singing something" in human beings,
male and female, of every race and national-
ity. This "singing something" is what makes
us *anthropos*, human beings. For Cooper, this
"singing something" (a synonym for divine
spark, *imago dei*) moves within every human
being and rises up against injustice to demand
freedom and equality.[13] As a relational womanist theologian, I would add that this "singing something" moves within every creature:
it is God in creation. Cooper's "irresistible

power not ourselves" is what womanists mean by "the Spirit" that dynamically creates, loves, and moves within creation. According to the Psalms, all of creation, the heavens and the earth, reveal the glory of God, the divine handiwork or imprint. Human beings are more complex creatures, yes, but not alone in revealing divine handiwork. In West African worldviews and in process metaphysics, the divine is present in human and nonhuman nature.

If this "singing something" or "irresistible power not ourselves" is present in and among us, then when we harm one another, we harm God. Womanist theologians have explored the relationship between the presence of God in creation and the violation of creation. Specifically, Delores Williams offers sociohistorical analysis of the "violation and exploitation of the land and of women's bodies," which has "led to the destruction of natural processes in nature." Williams analyses assaults upon nature, the human spirit, and the divine spirit, describing the "defilement of nature's body and of black women's bodies," particularly of workers in industry, as sin.[14] She examines the correlation between disrespect for the peoples of the earth, particularly African bodies, and disrespect for the earth. For Williams, when we violate black women's bodies and when we violate the earth, we sin against God. This is very similar to Marjorie Suchocki's process understanding of the fall to violence, which is sin against creation and sin against God.[15] In the understandings of both Williams and Suchocki, then, to lynch or crucify a black man, woman, or Jesus is always to lynch or crucify God. When Jesus was crucified, it was sin against creation and sin against God.

Christian, Pagan, or Follower of Jesus?

In *Jesus and the Disinherited* and *Head and Heart*, Howard Thurman writes of his journey to India to meet Mohandas Gandhi in the 1940s, when the United States was segregated and many black men were being lynched. Thurman was asked by a Hindu how he could be a Christian when this religion had oppressed so many people of color around the world in the name of God. The man said for Thurman to be a Christian made him a traitor to all the darker peoples of the earth (India, for example, had been colonized by the British who were Christian). Thurman responded, "I am a follower of Jesus,"[16] and he focused on the fact that Jesus was a poor Jew. Thurman was speaking and writing during a period when millions of Jews suffered and died at the hands of the Nazis. African Americans connect with this violence perpetrated by many so-called Christians, through the sociohistorical experiences of the millions of Africans thrown overboard during the trans-Atlantic slave trade; the brutal whippings, tortures, lynchings, and slayings of black bodies throughout the modern period; and the psychological torture of slavery and disinheritance.

African Americans find ourselves in paradox. What does it mean to love Jesus and his intimate relationship to God, who is Spirit, when Christianity as a Western institution has been so destructive toward people of color and women? Even Alice Walker, an avowed pagan, is clear that it is Christianity, with its history of conquest and oppression, that she finds troubling more than Jesus. In *Anything We Love Can Be Saved*, for example, she comments parenthetically, "(Everybody loved Jesus Christ. We recognized him as one of us, but a rebel and revolutionary, consistently speaking up for the poor, the sick, and the discriminated-against, and going up against the bossmen. . . . We knew that people who were really like Jesus were often lynched. . .)."[17]

Easter mornings in black churches have long been events of Passion not only because of the crucifixion of Jesus, but because of the memories of black people who were whipped at whipping posts and hung from trees. The understanding is that the world is a place of such hate and evil that it even hung God's own Son from a tree. If it happened to the Son of God, then it could happen to anyone in a world full of evil, especially those who are subject to oppressive powers. Walker writes, in reference to the "bossmen," that Jesus was killed by "the orthodox Jewish leaders and rich men of his day," which is inaccurate. He may have been killed by wealthy, ruling powers (Rome) but not by orthodox Jewish leaders. Walker is not a biblical scholar. Contemporary biblical scholars see Herod and Caiaphas not so much as "orthodox Jewish leaders" as much as pawns of a Roman empire entrusted to keep peaceful relationship within an empire subject to Caesar as god. It is Rome that persecuted rabbis like Jesus, not the Jews. Walker, like many unfamiliar with actual Jewish and Roman history, comes across as sounding anti-Jewish and anti-Semitic. This is not surprising, because most of us have inherited the same misinformation and must unlearn it. What is true about Walker's inherited understanding of Jesus is that he is very much like the lynched of the world. Jesus, like other rabbis during the period, was known to publicly resist the claims of an empire to be the divine kingdom and of an emperor to be god. There was nothing unusual about this belief in Judaism, orthodox or otherwise. Rome was threatened by any leader who relativized its power. What made Jesus and other rabbis who were crucified particularly problematic? Perhaps it was the claim to have power from God, power that only Caesar could have. Perhaps it was the spreading belief that Jesus was in God and God in Jesus, a heretical view for Rome if only Caesar could claim this. There is no doubt, however, that African Americans connect lynching with crucifixion, because both the lynched and the crucified defy the claims of empires no matter how small or large the empire may be, a sharecropping town in the deep Southern United States or an imperialistic nation.

Black Americans, male and female, love the God of Jesus, yet we are horrified by many of the things that have been done to us and others in the name of Western Christianity. We therefore challenge Western Christianity, always discerning "which Jesus" people are talking about when they claim to talk about Jesus as Christ. Is this Christ the Jesus that was crucified by the Romans, the Western empire that later claimed to be Christian but still fell in its claims to world power? Or is this Christ we are talking about the Jesus who was Mary's son, whom Peter knew, and about

whom Sojourner Truth preached powerfully
to others on her freedom journey with entire
communities? If the one we are talking about
is the former, then the speaker is an idola-
ter who does not really know Jesus, the one
Peter called Christ and Messiah. If the one we
are talking about is the latter, then this is the
one whose words challenged Rome's claim to
power through its false-god ruler Caesar, an
early signifier of worldly, political, economic,
and military might. This one, whose words
challenged the divinity of an emperor-god, is
the one in whom God lived just as he lived
in God. This is the one who brings deliverance, healing, freedom, and good news to the
poor, widows, orphans, the blind, the captive,
and most simply, to the least of these. This
Christ is not of Rome or of any worldly power.
This Christ is of *basileia tou theou,* the rule or
power of God, the power that transforms the
world, calling it into right relationship with
God's initial aim.

My understanding of Jesus the Christ is
different from Walker's. For Walker, Jesus,
"after Moses and Joshua . . . is the greatest
magician in the Bible"; similarly, Zora Neale
Hurston's *Moses Man of the Mountain* portrays Moses as a conjurer, like the shamans
of traditional African and African American
folk religions.[18] In biblical literature Jesus, like

Moses, is distinctive from shamans and magicians because Jesus worshipped the One God of Israel, the God of all creation according to the teachings attributed to Jesus. It is this God whom followers of Jesus worship and the Holy Spirit of this God to whom Jesus' followers pray to move in. It is this God that is the power of love that Walker finds so attractive in her native black culture. She writes, "It is fatal to love a God who does not love you. . . . Indeed, it was because the teachings of Jesus were already familiar to many of our ancestors, especially in the New World—they already practiced love and sharing that he preached—that the Christian Church was able to make as many genuine converts to the Christian religion as it did."[19]

Walker proposes that "all people deserve to worship a God who also worships them," one who "made them and likes them." Therefore, she concludes that "Nature, Mother Earth," is a good choice. I take Walker's commentary regarding "ancestral pagan" understandings of love in relation to Jesus' understanding of love in a very different direction. Like Walker, I appreciate the understanding, inherited from Africans and Native Americans, that God is not separate from nature or the body. It is possible to love nature, however, without worshipping it. Nature is evidence of divine, creative power

but not necessarily the power itself. If Walker
were a process metaphysician, one suspects
she would have the most in common with
Henry Nelson Wieman. For Wieman, a non-
theist, God *is* the natural, ever-creating processes of the universe. My own approach, like
that of Cobb and Suchocki, is theistic. I do not
doubt God's presence in creation, the sense
that it incarnates and reveals the sacred, or
the need to love it. That Rom. 8:22 describes
nature as awaiting human salvation for its
own redemption speaks to a Christian understanding of nature as sacramental, as being
in loving relationship with the divine in spite
of human acts of defilement. This is different,
however, from worshipping it. A sacrament
reveals the sacred but is never reduced to the
sacred. I question Walker's suggestion that
black people who worship the God of Jesus
worship nature instead. This does not make
sense if we ask certain questions.

If the love taught and embodied by Jesus is
the same love our ancestors knew, then *why
not* follow Jesus? Why should there not be
black worship of the God that Jesus incarnated as part of God's creating a new thing
in black religious practice and understanding? Moreover, if that love is fully embodied
in Jesus the Christ, then why refer to the God
of the Bible, of Moses, Joshua, and Jesus as

some "foreign" God? Our "pagan ancestors" were attracted to the power of this Son of God and son of Mary, Walker admits, because he was familiar. Jesus, Son of God and of a woman, was whipped and hanged from a tree, like the children of so many black mothers. Black people found power in Jesus, not simply out of shame about their old gods, but because Jesus spoke to their present situation in ways the old gods did not.

This God of Jesus is the God of love who moves throughout the ages. If this is Jesus' God, in whom Jesus lives and who lives in Jesus, then there is no need to replace Jesus with worship of earth and nature. The overarching biblical story cannot be reduced to the texts of violence that trouble Walker, but does the story of divine love of creation have the literal ultimate Word? Even Walker attests to the power of the Word of Love Jesus taught and embodied.[20] Yes, it is omnipresent in the earth that Walker worships and in the "Nature" that Walker believes is its Spirit, but it cannot be reduced to earth and nature.

In Walker's latest novel, *Now Is the Time to Open Your Heart*, the character Kate Talkingtree, whose voice seems to be largely based on Walker's, learns that the Earth Spirit or "Grandmother spirit" cannot be destroyed.[21] Talkingtree has long feared that we can destroy God by destroying the planet and its universe. Here Walker through Talkingtree comes close to recognizing that Spirit and nature are within each other but not the same. Therefore the Spirit cannot be destroyed, although we could destroy the universe, especially the planet Earth as we have come to know it. Walker writes of Talkingtree's conversation with the "Grandmother spirit": "First of all, abandon any notion that anything you humans do will ultimately destroy me. . . . There is no potion, no poison you can create, that will do anything but rearrange the pattern I have made. And, let me add, you were created in such a way that you can do this. So destruction too is part of the overall design."[22] This is very close to a process, relational understanding of God and the world. In process metaphysics we humans can only destroy creation as we know it, but not creation or the power of creativity as such. Walker needs to clarify in her work that God who is Spirit is not the cosmos or everything put *in* the cosmos or in all things. God is the energy or Spirit that produces matter, arranging it in many simple and complex patterns. From *The Color Purple* to *Now Is the Time to Open Your Heart*, Walker's characters have made pantheistic claims with occasional shifts to a panentheistic awareness. Her work frequently presents God as being all things or as creation, reflecting her ambivalence about the nature of God. It would be more precise, however, to say that God is omnipresent. This is a *panentheistic* claim, meaning that *God is present in all things, places, times, and beyond time*. This omnipresent God, who is Spirit, is the very power and life of the universe as we know it. God, who is Spirit, intimately connected to the matter of which "the world" is made, will simply create something else if we destroy "the world" as we know it.

A Christian womanist, process, relational cosmology opposes Walker's *pantheistic* claims, because if God *is* everything, then we can destroy God. Such a cosmology agrees with process metaphysicians that the Spirit will continue whether or not we destroy this planet and this universe as we have come to know it.[23] Walker's occasional awareness of Spirit as indestructible and everlasting is more accurate than her pantheistic claims. Moreover, if Walker's "Grandmother spirit" *is* "Nature" and "Earth" rather than omnipresent *in* nature, earth, and every other universe known, unknown, or yet to be created, then it is not the same as "the Spirit" of Christian faith. It is not the same Spirit, because the Spirit found in Jesus is the creator of all possible worlds, not just this one. Nonetheless, given the ambiguities of Walker's spirituality,

I would claim that sometimes Christian womanists are talking about the same Spirit and
sometimes not. The reader may wonder, "Why
engage Walker's work at all?" It is important
to engage her work, because regardless of the
points where Christian womanists may dis-
agree with her, she draws womanists' attention to the interconnectedness of Spirit and
creation, a relationship that our African ancestors did indeed know but that has been lost
to many through Western appropriations of
the teachings of Jesus. Having taken on such
destructive Western thinking patterns, some
African Americans have not been as proac-
tive as necessary about the water we drink,
the air we breathe, or the soil our food comes
from, even when it is killing us as a result of
present ecological crises. Jesus himself was in
very close relationship to the earth that sustained his body, as close to it as to the Spirit
that sustained his soul. This is evident from
the parables attributed to him and the prayer
of Jesus in which we are to ask of God that
"your will be done on earth as it is in heaven."
In God, there is no separation between heaven
and earth.

This follower of Jesus contends that God's
suffering, weeping, walking, eating, hearing,
speaking, loving, healing, and rejoicing in
Jesus' ministry to the oppressed peoples and

cosmos speaks to God's omnipresence in the universe. God experiences the oppressed in Jesus. Those who have experienced oppression often identify with Jesus the Christ, because Jesus in the New Testament identifies with the oppressed. Jesus' ministry is to the poor, the suffering, and the oppressed (Luke 4:16-20; Matt. 25:31ff.). Jesus suffers with the oppressed and knows their plight. Jesus is the very embodiment of God, Emmanuel, God with us, dust and spirit, human and divine, earthy like every human being yet different in the full incarnation of Spirit.

Jesus, who is dust and Spirit, matter and divine energy, prehends our joy and sorrow, our well-being and our suffering. Only God, who is Spirit, knows the world completely, as the world knows itself. Only God knows each event, individual, entity, or person fully. That Jesus had this type of knowledge speaks to Jesus' incarnation of Spirit. There is hope in the knowledge that God is compassionate, empathetic. God is passionate *with* us. God feels with us, lamenting in death and rejoicing in new life. Jesus' divine power of life continues to affect us in its loving response. For these reasons, it makes sense to follow Jesus while also challenging Western Christianity's relationship with oppressive, Western global economic power and expansion.

The Cross

Classical theologians have maintained that God is impassible and immutable, incapable of suffering, and unchanging. In maintaining this truth claim, however, they have never been able to make sense of Christ's full humanity and full divinity. They have traditionally turned to "mystery" in response to questions regarding divine incarnation.[24] The underlying concern for classical theologians is whether or not God died on the cross. If God is omnipotent (all-powerful), then God can neither die nor change. If God could suffer and die, the reasoning goes, then God would not be all-powerful.

The process-relational response is that God is not all-powerful. The fact that there are evil, suffering, and violence in the world indicates that if God is good and if God's initial aim is for the well-being of all creation, then God must share power. If God did not share power, then all would be well and we would not experience violence and suffering. Therefore God is not all-powerful. In history, we see evidence of events in which creation has experienced well-being, but we also see evidence of destruction and suffering. This indicates that there is freedom in the universe to participate or not to participate in God's initial aim for well-being. If there is freedom, then God shares power with the rest of creation.

Womanist theologians appeal to such freedom, uncover it, and act in it to free others. Some womanists are very traditional and are therefore uncomfortable with the concept of God as less than omnipotent. In process thought, however, God is still the most powerful, because God is everlasting and the very power of life, while creation in all of its present forms is finite in relation to divine creativity.

Jesus is embodied Spirit, embodied love and divine creativity, who overcomes evil, violence, suffering, and injustice. Jesus is dust and spirit. According to Gen. 2:5-7, to be human is to be made from the dust of the earth. Human beings are *adam,* earth creatures. We are of the earth, *adamah.*[25] What makes Jesus the Christ distinctive is his complete, earthy embodiment of divine goodness, love, and glory. God incarnate risks his life for the very love and freedom he embodies. God in Christ does this not as a sacrificial victim, but as one who overcomes evil, violence, suffering, and justice. Womanists seek to embody God like Jesus in their struggle for freedom, healing, and wholeness. Historically, black women like Harriet Tubman and Sojourner Truth have risked their lives in their struggle against evil, suffering, violence, and oppression.

Delores Williams argues that we need to move away from understandings of the atonement that emphasize sacrifice.[26] She believes this is necessary because historically women are among those who are most sacrificed. Women in abusive relationships, particularly in situations of domestic violence, have often wrongly been counseled to remain in dangerous relationships. The rationale is that sacrificial love and unmerited suffering are redemptive. This way of thinking has ended in death or near-death for many women. I and other womanist theologians argue that it is important to give attention to the cross to ensure that we stop the violence. We can preach the cross as a form of homeopathy, in which remembering the crucifixion of Jesus works to stop the violence rather than perpetuate it. In other words, with Christ we transform the cross into material for healing rather than destruction. The empty cross is a sign of resurrection, life, and hope.

We live in a world where hatred, hate crimes, and violence are rampant. We must never forget the cross, lest we repeat the violence that we seek to overcome. Williams argues that we ought to focus on the glory of God, found in the life and ministry of Jesus—the power of salvation that ushers in the reign of God. It is the power by which we overcome evil and suffering. We ought not to glorify evil and suffering in our struggle to overcome them, yet we cannot deny their historical and contemporary presence. Womanist theologians must take seriously the fact that few black women in America are willing to preach the life and ministry of Jesus without the cross. Jesus' victory on the cross gives black women courage to demand peace, freedom, equality, and authentic love. It is difficult to believe that black women will ever stop singing "The Blood That Jesus Shed for Me." We must consider why the cross is so important.

Protestant womanists have given little attention to Mary as *theotokos* or mother of God. Yet the question of Mary's relationship to Christ was very important for the early church writers. Along with womanist theologians like Williams, I am greatly interested in the understanding that some Korean women have of Mary. Williams is concerned that the virginity attributed to Mary as mother is something that ordinary mothers cannot identify with.[27] There is something even more important, however, to learn from Mary. So many Korean women and black American women, like Mary, have lost children, sons, and husbands to violence. From Mary's story Korean women learn to overcome the *han* experienced by such loss; African American women learn to overcome the *blues* experienced in such loss. Every Good Friday black American Christian women sing a song, "Were You There When They Crucified My Lord?" with plaintive voices. You can hear the moan in the women's voices as we remember not only Jesus' crucifixion, but the violent deaths of ancestors, elders, and loved ones in the past and in the present. Womanists need to explore the ways in which we are like Mary, who mourned her son's death but found resurrection, hope, and life.

If Mary were not the mother of God, then Christ's humanity would come into question. Was Christ fully human and fully divine or not? If Mary is not the mother of Christ, yet she conceived by the Holy Spirit, then Christ is fully divine but not fully human. For Nestorius, bishop of Constantinople in the early fifth century, Jesus was simply *theodochus,* the recipient of the divine Logos, the second person of the Trinity. Jesus is simply the vessel for the Logos in this scheme. There is a separation between, not an integration of, Christ's divinity and humanity. Nestorius's view was rejected by Cyril, bishop of Alexandria, and again at Chalcedon. The Council of Nicea formulated the creed in 325, the Council of Constantinople affirmed it in 381, and the Council of Chalcedon confirmed it in 451. The creed maintains that God is in Christ and

Christ is in God: Jesus the Christ, the Logos or Word of God, is God incarnate. Process-relational metaphysics helps make sense of what this means.

In a process-relational understanding, energy produces matter and matter produces energy. Likewise, spirit produces matter and matter produces spirit. So of course Jesus is matter and Spirit, divine and human, creature and creating, beloved and loving. Moreover, Mary is an integration of matter and spirit, and she experiences the full possibilities of bearing and raising a child who is the full embodiment of God, the all-inclusive power of life, abounding in love, and continuously creating and renewing. She is therefore an appropriate bearer of God, who is Spirit and who is embodied in Jesus the Christ, because God is omnipresent in creation. Mary at the cross witnesses the love and death of her own flesh and blood, because Jesus is flesh of her flesh and heart of her heart.

The blood shed on the cross takes on new meaning. It is Jesus' blood, it is Mary's blood, and it is the blood of Emmanuel, God with us. The heart pumps blood to give life. Life flows from God's heart to Mary's heart, to Jesus' heart, to all humanity. This God on the cross suffers with us in persecution and oppression. This resurrected God rejoices with us in vic-

tory over evil and suffering. Jesus' blood is
a symbol of abundant life and unsurpassable
love. In the Roman Catholic school I attended
as a child, the nuns always linked Jesus' love
with Mary's love as mother of God in Christ.
From them I learned about the sacred heart of
Jesus. Paintings of the sacred heart of Jesus as
well as paintings of Mary have influenced my
Christian consciousness, although I am Protestant. To preach Christ and him crucified, it
is necessary to focus on the heart of Jesus the
Christ and on the heart of Mary. This is a new
idea for Protestant womanists, but I believe
it is essential. Otherwise, we literally lose the
heart of the Christian message, and the relational understanding of womanist theology
becomes compromised.

When we consider the relationship of the
heart of God, who is Spirit, in relation to
Mary's own heart as she bears and raises a
son, Jesus, who is the Christ, then the Christian understanding of God's relationship to
the world becomes clearer. It is through the
heart of Jesus the Christ, son of Mary and son
of God, that we find dynamic, living, abundant hope and love to overcome violence and
suffering in the world. We are embraced in
the power of this unsurpassable love that permeates the universe, even when we are not
conscious of it. In this unsurpassable love,

we have hope for healing and abundant life. Is womanist theology the only theology that can do this? No, it is not, but womanist theology brings novel sociohistorical stories to the theological table. These stories bear witness to the power of love, life, and creativity embodied in Jesus Christ. We, too, are part of Christ's body with edifying stories to share. In Christ the witness of all earthling stories to the power of creative love become a living, multicolored quilt of dynamically shifting colors and patterns in the movement of the Spirit. The quilt of divine love draws humankind ever nearer into the healing warmth of God's mutual love and right relationship as an entire, ever-new creation.

6.

Passionate Living

Rosetta E. Ross

Another View of *The Passion*

The dogmatic view of Mel Gibson's *The Passion of the Christ* focused exclusively on Jesus' crucifixion as essential to Christian salvation. This view reflects the legacy of Judaism on which Christianity draws, particularly the practice of animal sacrifice in Hebrew scripture, and follows doctrinal developments of medieval Christian theology, particularly Anselm's satisfaction theory of atonement. Jesus' crucifixion, Christian dogmatism argues, reflects the necessity of blood sacrifice to accomplish the forgiveness of sins.[1] Evolving from this dogmatic belief in blood sacrifice and its accompanying focus on Jesus' crucifixion, the phrase "the Passion of Christ" has come to refer narrowly to those events ritually remembered as a part of the suffering and public execution Jesus experienced. These ritualized events include (but certainly are not limited to) Jesus' last meal with his disciples, his prayer in the garden of Gethsemane, his trial and condemnation, the scourging and crowning with thorns, the journey to Golgotha, the grief and support of Mary, his mother, his suffering on the cross, his death, and the piercing after his death. Some, but not nearly all, accounts of the Passion of Christ include the resurrection. In this case, admittedly the predominant view and long the traditional view, to speak of Jesus' Passion is to speak of his last days.

When defined less technically, *passion* pertains to emotional ardor, enthusiasm, rage, fervency, and even fire. Human passion is a reflection of deep feelings. If we think of passion in this more general manner, another way of examining Jesus' Passion is to consider what he lived for, what he seemed concerned most intensely about, what he was committed to. While it may be rightly argued that Jesus' condemnation and death themselves point to his deepest commitments, the contents of Jesus' commitments are not fully evident if we look only at the events of his last days. When Gospel accounts of the life

of Jesus are considered, his consistent and
passionate honoring of all persons as sacred
and his passionate advocating for a positive
quality of life[2] for all persons emerge as two
obvious deep commitments. Moreover, the
Gospels demonstrate that the weak, the poor,
and the socially dispossessed are especially
among those whom Jesus favored.[3] Recurring
stories of Jesus' miracles of healing, feeding
hungry crowds, and raising the dead—particularly during times when he had another
agenda—show Jesus' compassion for the sick,
hungry, and bereaved people he met. Jesus'
interactions with the woman caught in adultery, with the woman at the well, and with
Zaccheus the tax collector and his story about
the Samaritan who helps a wounded traveler
show Jesus' recognition of and concern for
people outside the mainstream. Jesus' words
about children and the poor and his acknowl-
edgment of a widow's small offering reflect
attention to the weak. His angry words and
actions toward traders in the temple and
leaders who took care of themselves at the
expense of their people show his deep concern for people who could not defend themselves. When Jesus' life is viewed as a model
for moral action, these commitments evident
in Jesus' life and ministry are shown to be
based on two principles: (1) moral teaching

and action should consistently recognize the dignity of all people, and (2) moral teaching and action should have the aim of bringing a positive quality of life to people, especially to the socially dispossessed.

Many activities Jesus engaged in and many principles Jesus taught caused conflict with political, social, and religious authorities. All four Gospel accounts of Jesus' life present him as an itinerant teacher-leader who was fully aware that his words and actions often displeased authorities. Those authorities eventually conspired against him. According to the Gospels, Jesus' passionate living brought on his death. That is, canonized narratives of Jesus' life indicate that his commitment to human dignity and to his vision of a better quality of life, especially for the dispossessed, caused his death. Among other things, then, Jesus' crucifixion reflects his living so passionately against the grain that the powers he encountered, the leaders and rulers of the day, felt it necessary either to silence Jesus or to fail to protect him, both of which contributed to his crucifixion.

Another doctrinal, but less strongly advocated, position within Christian tradition is the view that Jesus' life was a model of passionately committed living. To speak narrowly of Jesus' Passion by focusing exclusively on his

trial and death disconnects Jesus' being crucified for his deep feelings and commitments
from the actions and ministry that arose from
them. Defining the Passion narrowly also pre-
cludes careful and meaningful examination
of this aspect of Jesus' life. Certainly the passion of Jesus' ordinary living is not ritually
remembered. Perhaps most poignantly, the
constricted focus on Jesus' Passion as relating only to his last days leaves Christians
off the hook, without a ceremonial reminder
and, more significant, without responsibility
to follow Jesus' model in their ordinary lives.
Even within the tradition of weekly services,
during which a sermon or homily ostensibly
presents a reiteration of scripture, Christians—
particularly Protestants across the spectrum
of conservatives to liberals—do not experience
meaningful opportunities to ritualize reminders of the countercultural critique offered by
Jesus. What could be a major positive contribution by the tradition to society is lost.

Several theologians[4] recently have argued
that exclusive focus on the crucifixion detracts
from the meaning of Jesus' life and ministry
and from the this-worldly meaning of salvation. Like the pop cultural acronym WWJD
(What would Jesus do?), these theologians
lift up as significant the model of Jesus' life.
Moving beyond this cliché, however, these

theologians focus on the meaning of salvation and of Jesus' ministry for *living* persons who experience extreme deprivation and exclusion or who encounter intense opposition in the face of their good works. They argue that Jesus' life and ministry are far more life-giving than the cross in response to life-challenging experiences and to systems that often harm people. If the salvation that Christianity offers has anything to do with temporal (as well as with eternal) life, then, they suggest, the model of a Jesus who valued all people and who especially showed concern about marginal people's quality of life surely is worth considering.

When these theological views are taken into account, a general response to the question "What would Jesus do?" is that Jesus would teach and live in ways that lift people up and bring new life possibilities especially to the socially dispossessed. Using this question seems fruitful for Christian moral life when the general answer that guides particular actions is that Jesus would respond with passionate commitment to whatever circumstance or challenges he confronted. Jesus consistently responded passionately. The Gospels do not paint pictures of a Jesus who said "I'll think about it" or who pondered what would befall him if he took a particular course of action. On the contrary, Jesus' responses were not lukewarm;[5] they were immediate and passionately hot, reflecting his commitment to bring hope and change into persons' lives.

Finding Our Passion

Audre Lorde has written that we respect and honor ourselves when we appropriately seek to actualize the fullness of our deep feelings.[6] In her view, living passionately means living with integrity, having an internal sense of one's self and what one values. This does not mean living only for the self, however. Rather, Lorde argues for "deep participation" and "joint concerted actions" against suffering. Additionally, Lorde recognizes the possibility of acting intensely without regard for the self. Distinguishing such externally motivated action from actions emerging from internal values, she says that failure to be conscious of our own deepest feelings results in pornography, abuse, and absurdity.[7] Lorde's valuing of an internal source of authority, contrasted with acting on the basis of an external referent, is helpful in lifting up the countercultural critique that religious traditions can offer. Nevertheless, internal access to resources of religious traditions depends significantly on being shaped by and situated within the traditions. For this reason many people find maintaining relationship with religious communities of particular traditions as essential to identifying themselves as adherents of those traditions.

Following our passion may be a way of taking charge of and changing ourselves. This sometimes results in taking charge of and changing people, situations, and circumstances around us. When we do not respond to the passion within us, if we cannot imagine a course of action that reflects our deep feelings, we are left with no other vehicle for intense self-expression than to determine ways to align our actions with the paradigms that already exist.[8] Actively and critically situating ourselves within traditions over time may ignite our deepest feelings. It does not seem hyperbolic to say that for Jesus, being passionate was an ordinary way of living into his vision. The result, Christian tradition teaches, is that in spite of humble beginnings Jesus acted with such clear self-definition that generations of people, compelled by values he espoused, followed him. Many of Jesus' followers imagine the world being ordered differently, where each human life has dignity, and many followers act passionately to bring what they imagine into existence.

Following our deepest feelings generally means persisting in living against the grain. However, living with such commitment in our time may be viewed as overzealousness. Reinhold Niebuhr argued against the historical possibility of such altruism and said it "is dangerous because it encourages terrible fanaticisms."[9] One cannot overlook the damage and destruction caused by people who identify themselves as fervent followers of Jesus. Self-righteous zeal can be amazingly destructive. Moreover, distinguishing the "destructive" from the "constructive" zealot may be nearly impossible. Some critics will convincingly argue that the difference is no more than a matter of one's point of view. But there may be other possibilities for distinguishing the two. One way of considering a difference may be through consistent reference to what the Gospels present as two essential aspects in the content of Jesus' point of view. Examining the means and ends undertaken in one's actions presents a way of evaluating their consistency with two principles evident in Jesus' own passionate action. If honoring all persons as sacred was an essential aspect of Jesus' commitment to bringing a positive quality of life to people, especially to the socially dispossessed, then it is possible to identify general limits on the means that may be undertaken to reach the ends of new, better life. If honoring all persons as sacred is essential to the means of Christian practice, and if creating a positive quality of life especially for the marginalized is essential to the ends, then these principles can be a guide for Christian moral action; thus, being a true follower of Jesus would not be completely limited by the uncertainty of persistently seeking to avoid fanaticism or the destructive danger of self-referential and self-righteous zeal. For religious people generally, and Christians in particular, Thomas Holt calls acting in behalf of the self and the self's values "testimony and witness." Testimony, Hoyt says, is "public speech that is honest and empowering," and testimonies "keep alive a truth . . . that society often does not honor."[10] Among Christians, Jesus' life of commitment can be seen as this kind of testimony and witness to God's presence with him. An example from the Civil Rights Movement illustrates the possibility of a similar witness and testimony among ordinary persons.

The Example of Fannie Lou Hamer

Elsewhere I have explored the significance of religious identity to civil rights participation[11] as essential to understanding motivations of leaders and followers in the Movement. As an example of practice reflecting deep feeling and values, the activism of some civil rights participants also presents examples of following one's passion as informed by religious tradition. Fannie Lou Townsend Hamer is a paradigmatic example of a person who lived her passion through religious (particularly Christian) practice as a part of the Civil Rights Movement. Hamer's story yields at least three lessons: (1) values expressed in her activism coincide with the two principles of honoring the dignity of all people and creating a positive quality of life, especially for the socially dispossessed; (2) her activism was significant as an expression of deep feelings and values informed by her religious tradition; and (3) her activism expressed an integrity of the self reflected in an internalized sense of authority that contrasted sharply with then-contemporary social views.

Hamer's story is well-known. Fannie Lou Townsend (later Hamer) grew up in a share-cropping family in Mississippi, the youngest of twenty-two children. Entrapped in share-cropper indebtedness by age six, Fannie Lou persisted in that state well into her adult life. Because of her family's poverty and because of the nature of sharecropping culture, Fannie Lou achieved only six years of intermittent

education. At about age twenty-four Fannie
Lou Townsend met and married Perry Hamer,
also a sharecropper. They lived and worked
as a couple on the W. D. Marlowe Plantation
in Sunflower County, Mississippi, for at least
twenty years. Although it was two decades
after her marriage that Fannie Lou Hamer
encountered civil rights activism, her practices as timekeeper on the plantation reflected
values she lived out as a civil rights partici-
pant. Whenever possible, Hamer intervened
to prevent the plantation owner's defrauding
other sharecroppers, and she shared her family's limited resources with people who were
even more destitute.

In 1962, when Hamer was forty-four years
old, she attended a "civil rights meeting" and
soon became well-known for her tenacity in
pursuing civil rights work. She immediately
connected civil rights activism with her own
religious values and self-understanding and,
perhaps recognizing the profound opportunity
for self-realization, Hamer used Movement
practices to honor the dignity of other people
and improve the life circumstances of the poor,
to more fully and more passionately live out
her vision of how social life should be ordered,
and to express her own sense of integrity.

Thus, Hamer expressed values that coincide
with two principles from Jesus' life—honoring

the dignity of all persons and creating a positive quality of life especially for the socially
dispossessed—long before she encountered
civil rights activism. As a child she recognized
the dignity of people outside the mainstream
by questioning the legitimacy of difficulties
her mother experienced and of the share-
cropping system. Hamer considered difficult
life experiences and lack of access to material goods as incompatible with human dignity. She noted, for example, that her mother
patched "our clothes so we'd have something
to wear. And her own clothes—they'd been
patched and patched over so much till they
looked too heavy for her body to carry. All I
could think was why did it have to be so hard
for her." While still quite young, Fannie Lou
recognized the incongruity of what existed
with her belief in the dignity of all persons,
and she determined that "if I lived to get
grown and had a chance, I was going to try to
get something for my mother and I was going
to do something for the Black [people] of the
south if it would cost my life; I was determined to see that things were changed."[12]

Hamer identified the problem of dehumanizing black people through racial subordination as dehumanizing for all people. She
expressed appreciation for civil rights workers who came to her community because,

she said, "we had wondered if there was
anybody *human enough to see us as human
beings* instead of as animals."[13] Hamer's adult
expression of her childhood determination
underscored her respect for the dignity of all
persons and her concern especially to improve
the quality of life for people who experienced
the most difficulty. "I'm going to do all I can
for every oppressed person," she once said,
"because if I try to do something for one and
oppress the other, that is not right."[14] Her
work included projects as varied as leading
and agitating for broader political access that
resulted in dramatic increases in black civic
participation and founding a farm and hous-
ing cooperative program[15] that provided food
and home ownership for blacks and poor
whites and that helped change the face of
rural Mississippi by literally improving the
quality of many people's lives.

Fannie Lou Hamer's civil rights activism
expressed her deepest feelings and values
formed by her religious tradition. Although
Hamer often criticized black churches for
their failures, she also identified Christianity
as a part of black "heritage . . . a part of our
strength."[16] She frequently spoke of the relationship of her understanding of Christianity
and her values expressed in civil rights activism. "Christianity," Hamer once said, "is being

concerned about your fellow man, not building a million-dollar church while people are
starving right around the corner. Christ was a
revolutionary person, out there where it was
happening."[17] As Hamer reflected this understanding of herself and of Christianity in her
activism, she expressed an internal sense of
what was good that permitted her to act passionately—as Jesus did in his time—against the
grain of racial subordination. She also paid a
physical price for her passion. Once, when she
was returning from a voter education training in Georgia, local authorities so brutally
beat her that her skin and muscle tissue hard-
ened "like a piece of wood or somethin'."[18] As
Jesus did, so Fannie Lou Hamer suffered for
her witness and for living with such passion.
It is clear from Hamer's commitments that, for
her, living with passion was not the same as
living with suffering. Indeed, Hamer lived to
overcome suffering.

The same may be said of Jesus.

7.

The Passion and African American Pilgrimage

Robert M. Franklin

The film *The Passion of the Christ* stirred
wide interest and debate about the theological meaning of suffering. In an article
published just prior to its release, I specu-
lated that African American viewers would
identify profoundly with the "suffering servant" depicted therein.[1] Now, looking back,
I believe that the controversy and curiosity
about Christ's Passion may outlive the film's
shelf life by opening a window into African
American faith and history—a history that
every educated person should know.

Like most scholars and preachers, over the
years I have repeatedly received requests
from parents, pastors, and religious educators,
black and white, for a user-friendly approach

to thinking about the "big story" of African American history. I have often timidly suggested that they read the magisterial history text by John Hope Franklin (*From Slavery to Freedom*),[2] but I realized that they were asking for a brief, easy to remember, thumbnail sketch of our journey. I would like to use this opportunity to offer a basic sketch that can be used to convey the sweep of that history.

Story and Classic

Every people and culture possesses a story, a grand narrative. The purpose of the story is to set forth the origins of a people, their journey through time, and their current and future prospects. Whether conscious of it or not, we all are profoundly shaped by these myths. The word *myth* is the Greek word for story. It does not mean that the story is false; rather, the myth conveys truth to those who embrace it. As a character in Peter Shaffer's play *Equus* puts it, "we need a story to see in the dark."

So every culture has a story. Further, every culture possesses its own classics. Four things are noteworthy about classics.[3] First, classics are *pluriform*. They may be works of art, historical events, exemplary persons, or texts. Second, classics emerge from a particular culture but speak compellingly to all people. They are simultaneously *particular* and *universal*. You don't have to know the Russian language to appreciate Dostoevsky's profound insights into the human condition. You don't have to be Irish to apprehend the depth of understanding about human nature in James Joyce's works. You needn't be Italian to be overwhelmed by the masterful theological scope of Michelangelo's *Day of Judgment* in the Sistine Chapel. And you don't have to be African American to be grasped by the genius behind the work of Ralph Ellison or Zora Neale Hurston.

Third, the classic is distinguished from a period piece by its *timelessness*. Think of the great books that have shaped your life or your favorite piece of music. You can go back to them over and over and each time encounter something new. Theologian David Tracy has written that the classic possesses an "excess and permanence of meaning"[4] that renders it available to all rational people. Church historian Martin Marty says that you don't read the classic—it reads you.

I'm highlighting the concepts of story and classics for two reasons. First, one could say that each of us is a walking collection of stories and classics waiting to be discovered, read, and understood. It would be great fun to have a lunch conversation with a friend during which you both identify three books, films, pieces of music, and life experiences that make you who you are today. We all carry a few of the classics within us.

The African American Spiritual Pilgrimage

The African American story may be summarized as a drama in three parts: first, self-determination amid societal stability on the African continent; second, collective struggle amid the sorrows of slavery and Jim Crow segregation; and third, striving amid celebration and enjoyment of significant progress.

1. *Self-determination amid societal stability.* Part one of this story unfolds on the verdant and vast lands of Africa. It was and is a continent blessed with extraordinary natural resources. Use your imagination, and you can almost catch the aroma of coconut and banana, pineapple and pomegranates. The villages of central West Africa were highly organized and stable, and the people self-determined and proud. Historians like John Hope Franklin remind us that the village empires of Africa were smelting iron for tools and weapons while Asia and Europe lived in the Stone Age.

Thanks to their stability and social organization, villages expanded and prospered and grew into massive empires during the medieval period of the West. The empires of Ghana, Mali, and Songhay gave rise to the export and trade of African agricultural and manufactured products throughout the Mediterranean world, Middle East, and Asia. Monarchs throughout the world proudly displayed gold rings and exotic animal skins from the Gold Coast. As David Livingstone and Cecil Rhodes spread the word about Africa's abundance and majesty throughout the capitals of Europe, international curiosity about this strange and wonderful land heightened.

Over the centuries Africans received and cultivated a rich set of religious practices and beliefs that brought them into the presence of the holy. Although some Africans were acquainted with Christianity from the day of Pentecost onward, most West Africans embraced their own indigenous beliefs, which included belief in a high, supreme God, a sacred cosmology filled with lesser spirits and intermediaries, the use of drums to invite or conjure the presence of the holy, the conviction that there was no distinction between the sacred and the secular, the practice of sharing faith through oral traditions and story rather than a written text, and the fact that faith was a communal not an individual phenomenon.

With the dawn of the sixteenth century, Portugal, Holland, and Spain were rapidly expanding the trade of African men and women. The African chiefs and traders who conspired in this awful scheme could not have known that they were parties to one of the most horrific chapters in the world history of slavery. Nor could they have foreseen how the entire continent of Africa would be divided among seven European nations (Belgium, France, Germany, Great Britain, Italy, Portugal, and Spain) at an 1884 conference in Berlin. Thus ended the era of self-determination amid social stability, and a new chapter began.

2. *Collective struggle amid the sorrows of slavery.* Scholars commonly agree that slavery in what would become the United States began in 1619, when the first twenty Africans arrived in Jamestown, Virginia. At that time they were indentured servants who worked for seven years and were then permitted to go free, a practice known as manumission. This practice led to the growth of a free black population in the colonies. Manumission continued for four decades, until Virginia and Maryland passed laws making slavery a lifelong, permanent status. No longer would baptism and conversion enable freedom and enfranchisement. During these later years blacks endured sorrows and initiated a patient struggle to

reclaim self-determination. With the support of sympathetic whites and Native Americans, black people began to chip away at the moral and economic foundations of slavery. Slaves escaped, revolted, and organized to agitate for change. African people in America lived each day with the haunting uncertainty that their lives might be permanently changed in the blink of an eye. Husbands and sons could be lynched, mothers and daughters raped, children sold to another owner, and brutality visited upon anyone with the audacity to insist upon humane treatment.

But through it all the story evolved, and classics were born. Work songs composed to help people endure endless hours of monotonous, backbreaking work soon evolved into something unexpected: they began to absorb and express the inner lives of African slaves. Their rage and resentment as well as their faith, hope, and love fused into the classics we know as the Negro spirituals. These songs capture much of the sadness, sorrow, hope, and joy of black people as they viewed their suffering through the lens of a suffering God. They found in the Jesus who cried "My God, why hast thou forsaken me?" a limited but divine figure who showed them the importance of honesty about their sense of abandonment by and estrangement from God.

That same inner spiritual fortitude bore institutional manifestations as the independent black churches were founded. Even in slavery black people expressed self-determination as they refused to endure the humiliations of worshiping in the rear pews or balconies of the master's church and instead started their own churches. In 1773 the first African Baptist Church was established in South Carolina. Later the congregation moved to Savannah, and today it is regarded as the oldest continuous black congregation in America. Its founding dates of 1773–75 underscore the claim that the black church preceded the birth of the American republic. In the 1780s African Methodist Episcopal churches followed in Philadelphia and New York. For more about this important history, consult Gayraud Wilmore's wonderful book, *Black Religion and Black Radicalism*.[5]

The proliferation of black institutions extended beyond planting black churches. In 1855 only two colleges were devoted to the higher education of blacks, Wilberforce University and Lincoln University of Pennsylvania. A hundred years later, there were over one hundred schools. Just after the Civil War a great number of the historically black colleges and universities were established. I attended Morehouse College in Atlanta, where

I had the privilege of being surrounded and embraced by the many schools of the Atlanta University Center, the largest concentration of black higher educational institutions in the world. For all those who attend black colleges, no matter where they are, it is liberating and empowering to reflect on the collective achievements, intellectual power, and potential of these institutions.

These schools nurtured the scientific and agricultural genius of people like George Washington Carver, who was born a slave and went on to teach at Tuskegee Institute. He made an impact on the South's economy as he persuaded farmers to end their reliance on cotton, which depleted the land, and urged them to switch to nutrient-rich, soil-renewing crops like peanuts and sweet potatoes. Carver then developed hundreds of money-making by-products from these crops; he also invented products that automobile magnate Henry Ford used and adapted for his industry.

Madame C. J. Walker became the nation's first black female millionaire as she manufactured and then marketed door-to-door skin and hair care products in Indianapolis. She was an early precursor to Oprah Winfrey, who *Fortune* magazine lists as the world's only black female billionaire.

In the 1920s the Harlem Renaissance brought to the world new classics in literature, music, art, and politics. The musical works of Scott Joplin, Louis Armstrong, Duke Ellington, Bessie Smith, Fats Waller, Billie Holiday, Sarah Vaughn, and Ella Fitzgerald added to the growing list of cultural classics. These artists joined the ranks of writers such as Langston Hughes, Countee Cullen, Zora Neale Hurston, Paul Laurence Dunbar, James Baldwin, and Richard Wright.

This period of collective struggle and progress was met with a fierce and violent resistance from various domestic terrorist organizations such as the Knights of the Ku Klux Klan. The King Center and Emory University a few years ago sponsored a photography exhibit in Atlanta titled "Without Sanctuary," which documented the fact that between 1882 and 1901 over a hundred lynchings occurred each year—almost all of the victims were black. This fueled the migration of blacks in a two-stage pattern from the rural South to the urban South and from the urban South to cities in the North.

Leading the intellectual charge to eradicate domestic terror and the vast legal matrix of segregation were intellectual and legal wizards like W. E. B. DuBois, Thurgood Marshall, Ida B. Wells, and A. Philip Randolph. In the end it was the emergence of television and mass media that ensured that the story of the freedom struggle and the sorrows of racial injustice reached a distant America. According to sociologist Aldon Morris, in 1953 only 45 percent of American households owned televisions. Five years later 83 percent owned them. At the same time the evening news format expanded from fifteen to thirty minutes. Suddenly, for the first time in American history, everyone could tune in and see firsthand what was happening on the far side of the world—places like Montgomery, Alabama, and Little Rock, Arkansas. Morris reminds us that what they saw was young Martin Luther King Jr., a black Baptist preacher with a PhD from Boston who quoted Shakespeare and Aristotle along with Thomas Jefferson and the prophet Amos. Dressed in a dark suit and starched white shirt, King made "good copy," and the media loved him. Ultimately, it was his persona and television's craving for charisma that boosted the Civil Rights Movement into another galaxy of efficacy.

Just as the slave trade interrupted the stability and self-determination of Africans, the progress and hopefulness King embodied were dramatically interrupted by violence on April 4, 1968, when King was murdered, but not without the moral and legal victories of a new Civil Rights Act, Voting Rights Act, and a president committed to enforcing them.

During that period, the movement marched to the beat of new sounds provided by the gospel music of Mahalia Jackson and Tommy Dorsey and also the magical sounds of Motown. Is there anyone reading this who has not been moved and deeply shaped by these classics?

3. *Striving amid celebration.* This is the part of black history that is the shared experience of all good and decent Americans. This part of the story occurs in the context of a diverse and pluralistic nation that is willing to listen, learn, celebrate, and cooperate to build a stronger nation and world.

But there is much striving ahead for us if we are to make the American dream real for our fellow citizens.

- One in four American children lives in poverty; one in two is a minority kid.
- In 1980 there were 320,000 people in America's prison system; today there are over two million.
- Thirty percent of young black men have been in prison or are under the supervision of the criminal justice system, while only 18 percent have attended college.
- Poor women spend 25 percent of their income on child care, while affluent women spend 6 percent.

- About 68 percent of African American births are nonmarital births.

Indeed, there is much work and striving ahead, but there is much to celebrate as well.

- In 1970, 58 percent of blacks between the ages of twenty-five and thirty-five had completed high school, compared with 77 percent of whites. In 1990, 82 percent of blacks completed high school, compared with 89 percent for whites.
- In 1970, only 7 percent of blacks had four or more years of college, compared with 17 percent for whites. In 1990, 12.7 percent of blacks had completed college, compared with 24 percent of whites.

Some gaps are closing, and the progress made so far must inspire us to achieve more.

We Must Be Transformed Nonconformists

The Passion phenomenon can be a symbol that points us to the history of African Americans. Most Americans know nothing of African American history, and, if we are honest, an alarming number of young black people know very little about their own story and people. In the portrait of the suffering Christ, the God who hurts and is broken for others, we may glimpse the history of a people who walked out of Eden into Mother Africa, only to find the horrors of hell in North America. But today they are regaining paradise lost.

All Americans—all people—can celebrate the contributions of neurosurgeon Ben Carson, the stereotype crushing power of "The Cosby Show," the global leadership of Colin Powell, the heart-stopping magic of Michael Jordan and Tiger Woods, the business acumen of Richard Parsons of Time Warner and Ken Chenault of American Express, and the less famous but ever important steadfastness, sacrifice, and hope of everyday people. All these remind us of the possibility of triumph and resurrection after the agony of abandonment and estrangement.

But let us do more than learn black history: let us allow that history to inspire moral agency in every one of us. Heed Dr. King's invitation in his sermon "Transformed Nonconformists": "This hour in history needs a dedicated circle of transformed nonconformists. The saving of our world from pending doom will come not from the action of a conforming majority, but through the creative maladjustment of a transformed minority."[6]

And while we take up the mantle of moral agency or transformed nonconformism, let us also expand our consciousness as universal people by internalizing an expanding canon of classics, so that we will learn our story and know the story of humanity. Then we can appreciate the challenging words often attributed to Rabbi Hillel: "The world is equally balanced between good and evil. Your next act will tip the scale."

Notes

Preface

1. Lord of the Crucified

1. James H. Cone, *God of the Oppressed* (New York: Seabury, 1975).

2. Gayraud S. Wilmore, *Black Religion and Black Radicalism: An Interpretation of the Religious History of Afro-American People*, 2nd ed. (Maryknoll, N.Y.: Orbis, 1983).

3. Matthew Johnson, "Black Theology," in *The Encyclopedia of Religion*, 2nd ed., ed. Lindsay Jones (Detroit: Macmillan Reference, 2005).

4. See, for example, Cecil Wayne Cone, *The Identity Crisis in Black Theology* (Nashville: AMEC, 1975), and Charles H. Long, *Significations: Signs, Symbols, and Images in the Interpretation of Religion* (Philadelphia: Fortress Press, 1986).

5. Jürgen Moltmann, *The Crucified God: The Cross of Christ as the Foundation and Criticism of Christian Theology*, trans. R. A. Wilson and John Bowden (Minneapolis: Fortress Press, 1993 [1974]), 45–46.

6. Victor E. Frankl, *Man's Search for Meaning: An Introduction to Logo Therapy*, 3rd ed. (New York: Simon & Schuster, 1984).

7. William Storm, *After Dionysus: A Theory of the Tragic* (Ithaca, N.Y.: Cornell University Press, 1998).

8. See also Paul Tillich, *Systematic Theology*, 3 vols. (Chicago: University of Chicago Press, 1951), 1:61–62.

9. Theophus H. Smith, *Conjuring Culture: Biblical Formations of Black America* (New York: Oxford University Press, 1994), 143.

10. Cone, *God of the Oppressed*.

11. Moltmann, *The Crucified God*, 48.

12. Irene Smith Landsman, "Crises of Meaning in Trauma and Loss," in Jeffrey Kauffman, ed., *Loss of the Assumptive World: A Theory of Traumatic Loss* (New York: Brunner-Routledge, 2002), 28.

13. See Howard Thurman, *Deep River and The Negro Spiritual Speaks of Life and Death* (Richmond, Ind.: Friends United Press, 1975); W. E. B. DuBois, *The Souls of Black Folk* (New York: Knopf, 1993); Lawrence W. Levine, *Black Culture and Black Consciousness: Afro-American Folk Thought from Slavery to Freedom* (New York: Oxford University Press, 1977); Lerone Bennett, *The Black Mood and Other Essays* (New York: Barnes & Noble, 1970).

14. Levine, *Black Culture*, 39.

15. DuBois, *Souls of Black Folk*, 151.

16. Thurman, *The Negro Spiritual*, 111.

17. Martin Hengel, *Crucifixion: In the Ancient World and the Folly of the Message of the Cross* (Philadelphia: Fortress Press, 1977), 34.

18. Fannie Lou Hamer, quoted in Stewart Burns, *To the Mountaintop: Martin Luther King Jr.'s Sacred Mission to Save America, 1955–1968* (New York: HarperCollins, 2004), 244.

19. Thurman, *The Negro Spiritual*, 26.

20. Storm, *After Dionysus*, 86.

21. See, for example, Clifton H. Johnson, ed., *God Struck Me Dead: Voice of Ex-Slaves* (Cleveland: Pilgrim, 1993).

22. Charles B. Strozier, "Heinz Kohut's Struggles with Religion, Ethnicity, and God," in Janet Liebman Jacobs and Donald Capps, eds., *Religion, Society, and Psychoanalysis: Readings in Contemporary Theory* (Boulder: Westview, 1997), 171.

23. Ibid., 170.

24. Moltmann, *The Crucified God*, 48.

25. N. Katherine Hayles, *The Cosmic Web: Scientific Field Models and Literary Strategies in the Twentieth Century* (Ithaca, N.Y.: Cornell University Press, 1984), 175.

26. Ibid., 175–76.

27. Ibid., 175.

28. Pfeffer, *Nietzsche*, 238.

2. Were You There?

1. George M. Marsden, *Fundamentalism and American Culture: The Shaping of Twentieth-Century Evangelicalism, 1870–1925* (New York: Oxford University Press, 1980), 92.

2. Cited in ibid., 92.

3. Rudolf Otto, *The Idea of the Holy: An Inquiry into the Non-Rational Factor in the Idea of the Divine and Its Relation to the Rational*, 2nd ed., trans. John W. Harvey (New York: Oxford University Press, 1958).

4. Richard J. Powell, *Homecoming: The Art and Life of William H. Johnson* (New York: Rizzoli International, 1991), 182–84.

5. Olaudah Equiano, *The Life of Olaudah Equiano, or Gustavus Vassa, the African* (New York: Dover, 1999), 33.

6. Albert J. Raboteau, *Slave Religion: The "Invisible Institution" in the Antebellum South* (New York: Oxford University Press, 1978), 126.

7. Howard Thurman, *Jesus and the Disinherited* (Boston: Beacon, 1996 [1949]).

8. Raboteau, *Slave Religion*, 236.

9. Martin Hengel, *The Atonement: The Origins of the Doctrine in the New Testament* (Philadelphia: Fortress Press, 1981), 42.

10. Mamie Bradley cited in Juan Williams, *Eyes on the Prize: America's Civil Rights Years, 1954–1965* (New York: Penguin, 1988), 44.

11. Alister E. McGrath, *Luther's Theology of the Cross: Martin Luther's Theological Breakthrough* (New York: Blackwell, 1985).

3. What Manner of Love?

1. Jennie Evelyn Hussey, "Lead Me to Calvary," in *The African American Heritage Hymnal* (Chicago: Gia, 2001 [1921]).

2. The collective affirmation of Christ's a priori love is found in 1 John 4:19: "We love [him] because he first loved us."

3. The most contemporary of the theorists, Gustaf Aulén (1879–1977) proffered an account of the Atonement that he deemed most faithful to the worldviews of the biblical era in *Christus Victor: An Historical Study of the Three Main Types of the Idea of the Atonement* (New York: Macmillan, 1969).

4. A benediction commonly used and embroidered upon in black church settings.

5. This is a popular refrain in many songs in black Pentecostal settings, perhaps an adumbration of the hymn, "'Tis So Sweet to Trust in Jesus" by Louisa M. R. Stead.

6. See Martin Luther King Jr., *Strength to Love* (Philadelphia: Fortress Press, 1981 [1963]); Reinhold Niebuhr, *The Nature and Destiny of Man* (New York: Scribner's Sons, 1943); Cornel West, *Race Matters* (Boston: Beacon, 1993).

7. Niebuhr, *Nature and Destiny*, 78. Radical blacks of the 1960s made up a little ditty deriding black people's adherence to the love ethic: "Too much love, too much love, nothing kills a n----r like too much love." See August Meier et al., eds., *Black Protest Thought in the Twentieth Century* (New York: Macmillan, 1971); Alex Poinsett, "The Quest for a Black Christ," *Ebony*, March 1969; and Albert Cleage, *The Black Messiah* (New York: Sheed and Ward, 1968).

8. James H. Cone, *Black Theology and Black Power* (Maryknoll, N.Y.: Orbis, 1997 [1969]), and *A Black Theology of Liberation* (Maryknoll, N.Y.: Orbis, 1986 [1970]).

9. Ps. 48:14: "For this God is our God for ever and ever; he will be our guide even unto death" (King James Version).

10. See Robert E. Hood, *Begrimed and Black: Christian Traditions on Blacks and Blackness* (Minneapolis: Fortress Press, 1994), and *Must God Remain Greek? Afro Cultures and God Talk* (Minneapolis: Fortress Press, 1990). See also Cain Hope Felder, *Troubling Biblical Waters: Race, Class, and Family* (Maryknoll, N.Y.: Orbis, 1989).

11. See Delores S. Williams, *Sisters in the Wilderness: The Challenge of Womanist God-Talk* (Maryknoll, N.Y.: Orbis, 1993). Williams distinguishes between coerced surrogacy (of slavery) and voluntary surrogacy to describe the character of black women's oppression in the post-slavery workforce.

12. The late James Melvin Washington, former professor of Church History at Union Theological Seminary (New York) spoke these words to me in a private conversation a year before his untimely death in 1997. See the book he edited, *Conversations with God: Two Centuries of Prayers by African Americans* (New York: HarperCollins, 1994).

13. Jacquelyn Grant, "Epistle to the Black Church: What a Womanist Would Want to Say to the Black Church," *AME Church Review* (April–June 1991).

14. See Kelly Brown Douglas, *The Black Christ* (Maryknoll, N.Y.: Orbis, 1994); Jacquelyn Grant, *White Women's Christ, Black Women's Jesus: Feminist Christology and Womanist Response* (Atlanta: Scholars Press, 1989); Delores S. Williams, "Black Women's Surrogacy Experience Challenges Traditional Notions of the Atonement," in Paula M. Cooey, William R. Eakin, and Jay B. McDaniel, eds., *After Patriarchy: Feminist Transformations of the World's Religions* (Maryknoll, N.Y.: Orbis, 1991); and JoAnne Marie Terrell, *Power in the Blood? The Cross in the African American Experience* (Maryknoll, N.Y.: Orbis, 1998).

15. See Matt. 24:34; Luke 11:50; John 17:24; Eph. 1:4; Heb. 9:20; 1 Peter 1:20; Rev. 13:8.

16. Carl E. Braaten and Robert W. Jenson, eds., *Christian Dogmatics*, 2 vols. (Philadelphia: Fortress Press, 1984), 2:65.

17. Ibid.

18. *Sin as violation* is comparable to what Delores Williams has called *sin as defilement,* which can be applied to concerns for ecosystems as well as for persons and groups. I am using the term *violation* because of its etymological relationship to the word *violence,* apropos this study, and because it suggests a wider range of attitudes and actions, for example, from coveting to encroachment to trespass to defilement.

19. Terrell, *Power in the Blood?* 124.

20. Ibid.

21. Kenzaburo Oe, *Hiroshima Notes,* trans. Toshi Yonezawa, ed. David L. Swain (Tokyo: YMCA Press, 1981).

4. Identifying with the Cross of Christ

1. A. O. Scott, "Good and Evil Locked in Violence Showdown," *New York Times,* February 25, 2004.

2. Lawrence Toppman, "Passion: One Man's Potent, Bloody Vision," *Charlotte Observer,* February 25, 2004, 1A.

3. Traditional spiritual cited in Albert J. Raboteau, *Slave Religion: The "Invisible Institution" in the Antebellum South* (New York: Oxford University Press, 1978), 259.

4. Traditional spiritual cited in James H. Cone, *The Spirituals and the Blues* (Maryknoll, N.Y.: Orbis, 1972), 22.

5. Ibid., 47–49.

6. James Cone, *God of the Oppressed* (San Francisco: Seabury, 1975).

7. Cone, *Spirituals,* 48.

8. Cone, *God of the Oppressed,* 112.

9. Ibid., 125.

10. Cone, *Spirituals*, 48.

11. Raboteau, *Slave Religion*, 250.

12. Cone, *Spirituals*, 48–49.

13. Reverdy C. Ransom, "The Paraclete of God" in Anthony B. Pinn, *Making the Gospel Plain: The Writings of Bishop Reverdy C. Ransom* (Harrisburg, Pa.: Trinity Press International, 1999), 169.

14. Daniel Alexander Payne, "Welcome to the Ransomed," in Milton C. Sernett, ed., *African American Religious History: A Documentary Witness* (Durham, N.C.: Duke University Press, 1999), 235.

15. Raboteau, *Slave Religion*, 235.

16. Langston Hughes, "A New Song," in *The Collected Poems of Langston Hughes*, ed. Arnold Rampersad (New York: Vintage, 1995), 170.

17. Anthony B. Pinn, *Why Lord?: Suffering and Evil in Black Theology* (New York: Continuum, 1995), 89.

18. Pinn, *Why Lord?* 111.

19. Delores S. Williams, "A Crucifixion Double Cross?" *The Other Side* (September–October 1993): 25–26.

20. Delores S. Williams, *Sisters in the Wilderness: The Challenge of Womanist God-Talk* (Maryknoll, N.Y.: Orbis, 1993), 161–70.

21. Williams, "Crucifixion Double Cross?" 26.

22. Ibid., 27.

23. Amos Jones, *Paul's Message of Freedom: What Does it Mean to the Black Church?* (Valley Forge, Pa.: Judson, 1984), 196.

24. Neil Elliot, "The Anti-Imperial Message of the Cross," in Richard A. Horsley, ed., *Paul and Empire: Religion and Power in Roman Imperial Society* (Harrisburg, Pa.: Trinity Press International, 1997), 167.

25. Charles B. Cousar, *A Theology of the Cross: The Death of Jesus in the Pauline Letters* (Minneapolis: Fortress Press, 1990), 21.

26. Demetrius K. Williams, *Enemies of the Cross of Christ: The Terminology of the Cross and Conflict in Philippians* (Sheffield: Sheffield Academic Press, 2002), 25.

27. Demetrius K. Williams, "The Terminology of the Cross and the Rhetoric of Paul," in *The Society of Biblical Literature Seminar Papers 1998* (Atlanta: SBL Press, 1998), 677–99.

28. J. C. Beker, *Paul the Apostle: The Triumph of God in His Life and Thought* (Philadelphia: Fortress Press, 1980), 199.

29. See Demetrius K. Williams, "Paul's Anti-Imperial Discourse of the Cross: The Cross and Power in 1 Corinthians 1–4," in *Society of Biblical Literature Seminar Papers 2000* (Atlanta: SBL Press, 2000), 796–823; Neil Elliot, "Anti-Imperial Message," and his *Liberating Paul: The Justice of God and the Politics of the Apostle* (Maryknoll, N.Y.: Orbis, 1994); and Richard A. Horsley, *Paul and Empire*.

30. Richard A. Horsley and Neil Asher Silberman, *The Message and the Kingdom: How Jesus and Paul Ignited a Revolution and Transformed the Ancient World* (Minneapolis: Fortress Press, 1997), 54.

31. Elliot, "Anti-Imperial Message," 167.

32. Ibid, 183.

33. Ibid., 182.

34. Cone, *God of the Oppressed*, 33.

35. James H. Cone, *A Black Theology of Liberation* (Philadelphia: Lippincott, 1970), 27.

36. Ibid., 200.

37. Cone, *God of the Oppressed*, 191–93.

38. Raboteau, *Slave Religion*, 305.

39. William A. Andrews, ed., *Sisters of the Spirit: Three Black Women's Autobiographies of the Nineteenth Century* (Bloomington: Indiana University Press, 1986), 292.

40. Reverdy C. Ransom, "The Future of the Negro in the United States, " in Pinn, *Making the Gospel Plain*, 248–49.

41. Reverdy C. Ransom, "The Race Problem in a Christian State, 1906," in *African American Religious History*, 337–38.

42. Quoted in Cheryl Townsend Gilkes, *If It Wasn't for the Women: Black Women's Experience and Womanist Culture in Church and Community* (Maryknoll, N.Y.: Orbis, 2001), 123; original source: Charles H. Pleas, *Fifty Years Achievement (History): Church of God in Christ* (Memphis: Church of God in Christ Publishing House, n.d. [ca. 1975]), 35.

43. Martin Luther King Jr., speaking at Reidsville State Prison, Tattnall County, Georgia, October 26, 1960, cited in David J. Garrow, *Bearing the Cross: Martin Luther King, Jr. and the Southern Christian Leadership Conference* (New York: Vintage, 1988), opposite copyright page.

44. Martin Luther King Jr., speaking at the National Conference on Religion and Race, Chicago, Illinois, January 17, 1963, cited in Garrow, *Bearing the Cross*, opposite copyright page.

45. Martin Luther King Jr., "Suffering and Faith," in James Melvin Washington, ed., *A Testament of Hope: The Essential Writings of Martin Luther King, Jr.* (San Francisco: Harper & Row, 1986), 42.

46. Martin Luther King Jr., "Letter from a Birmingham Jail," in *A Testament of Hope*, 298.

47. Martin Luther King Jr., "Nonviolence and Racial Justice," in *A Testament of Hope*, 9.

48. Martin Luther King Jr., speaking at Penn Community Center, Frogmore, South Carolina, May 22, 1967, cited in Garrow, *Bearing the Cross*, opposite copyright page.

49. JoAnne Marie Terrell, *Power in the Blood? The Cross in the African American Experience* (Maryknoll, N.Y.: Orbis, 1998), 142.

5. Womanist Passion

1. Working title for a book on the dance of the Trinity, forthcoming in 2005 from Chalice Press.

2. Alice Walker, *In Search of Our Mothers' Gardens: Womanist Prose* (New York: Harcourt Brace Jovanovich, 1983), xi.

3. Ibid.

4. Charles Hartshorne, *Omnipotence and Other Theological Mistakes* (Albany: State University of New York Press, 1985), 14.

5. Karen Baker-Fletcher, *A Singing Something: Womanist Reflections on Anna Julia Cooper* (New York: Crossroad, 1994).

6. John B. Cobb Jr. and David Ray Griffin, *Process Theology: An Introductory Exposition* (Philadelphia: Westminster, 1976), 49, 52–54.

7. Marjorie Suchocki, *God, Christ, Church: A Practical Guide to Process Theology* (New York: Crossroad, 1992), 1, 88–90, 98, 105–6, 117–25.

8. Hartshorne, *Omnipotence*, 14, 45, 86; idem, *The Divine Relativity: A Social Conception of God* (New Haven, Conn.: Yale University Press, 1948), 46.

9. Alfred North Whitehead, *Process and Reality: An Essay in Cosmology*, corr. ed., ed. David Ray Griffin and Donald W. Sherburne (New York: Free Press, 1978 [1929]), 343–44, 351.

10. See Cobb and Griffin, *Process Theology*, 19–22, 120–27; Suchocki, *God, Christ, Church*, 1–13, 28–36, 57, 202–3, 243.

11. Cobb and Griffin, *Process Theology*, 49.

12. Baker-Fletcher, *A Singing Something.*

13. Ibid.

14. Delores S. Williams, "Sin, Nature, and Black Women's Bodies," in Carol Adams, ed., *Ecofeminism and the Sacred* (New York: Continuum, 1993), 24–29.

15. Marjorie Suchocki, *The Fall to Violence: Original Sin in Relational Theology* (New York: Continuum, 1995).

16. Howard Thurman, *Jesus and the Disinherited* (Richmond, Ind.: Friends United Press, 1981), 13–35; idem, *With Head and Heart: The Autobiography of Howard Thurman* (San Diego: Harvest, 1981 [1979]).

17. Alice Walker, "The Only Reason You Want to Go to Heaven Is That You Have Been Driven Out of Your Mind," in *Anything We Love Can Be Saved* (New York: Random House, 1997), 18.

18. Ibid. See also Zora Neale Hurston, *Moses, Man of the Mountain* (New York: HarperCollins, 1991).

19. Walker, *Anything We Love Can Be Saved*, 25.

20. I am obviously basing my argument on Johannine and early Christian understandings, particularly in the writings of Athanasius, of Jesus as *Logos*, meaning "word" or "knowledge." It is

associated with wisdom. See John 1:1 in any translation of the New Testament. See also Athanasius, *Orations against the Arians,* Book 1, in William G. Rusch, ed. and trans., *The Trinitarian Controversy,* Sources of Early Christian Thought (Philadelphia: Fortress Press, 1980), 87–88. See also Alice Walker, *Living by the Word: Selected Writings, 1973–1987* (New York: Harcourt Brace Jovanovich, 1980), 1–2. Walker's understanding of what it means to "live by the Word" comes from a dream of a "two-headed woman," or root worker, whom she believes to be a healer and a wise woman. In the dream, the woman told Walker to "live by the Word and keep walking." I am deliberately contrasting Walker's understanding with a specifically Christian understanding in which Jesus the Christ is the Word, the Logos, the very knowledge that is with God at creation. For a Christian womanist, living by the Word means to walk with Jesus. In Walker's work the meaning is deliberately vague, and it may very well be something else entirely. My argument here is that if Jesus' message of love is true as Walker acknowledges, then there is no good reason *not* to follow the living Word or Logos incarnate in Jesus. My goal here is not to "make" Walker Christian or a follower of Jesus, but to note some of the ambivalence in her work regarding black people who follow Jesus and the contradictions in her work regarding the value of biblical literature.

21. Alice Walker, *Now Is the Time to Open Your Heart* (New York: Random House, 2004), 77–78.

22. Ibid.

23. For the process arguments on which this is based, see John B. Cobb Jr., *Sustaining the*

Common Good: A Christian Perspective on the Global Economy (Cleveland: Pilgrim, 1994).

24. Hartshorne, *Omnipotence*, 51–63. John B. Cobb Jr., *Christ in a Pluralistic Age* (Philadelphia: Westminster, 1975), 136–46. See also Cobb and Griffin, *Process Theology*, 96–106.

25. See Karen Baker-Fletcher, *Sisters of Dust, Sisters of Spirit: Womanist Wordings on God and Creation* (Minneapolis: Fortress Press, 1998), 17–19.

26. Delores S. Williams, *Sisters in the Wilderness: The Challenge of Womanist God-talk* (Maryknoll, N.Y.: Orbis, 1993), 161–67.

27. Ibid., 179–84.

6. Passionate Living

1. In addition to Judaism and atonement theology, Christian scripture, especially Hebrews 9, argues for the requirement of blood sacrifice for forgiving sins (see especially v. 22).

2. Delores Williams uses the term *positive quality-of-life* to identify what she calls Jesus' "ministerial vision." See Delores S. Williams, *Sisters in the Wilderness: The Challenge of Womanist God-Talk* (Maryknoll, N.Y.: Orbis, 1993).

3. Recent theological developments, especially liberation theologies, significantly demonstrate that the Christian canon portrays Jesus' ministry as particularly focused on social outsiders.

4. See, for example, Williams, *Sisters in the Wilderness*; JoAnne Marie Terrell, *Power in the Blood? The Cross in the African American Experience* (Maryknoll, N.Y.: Orbis, 1998); J. Denny Weaver, *The Nonviolent Atonement* (Grand Rapids: Eerdmans, 2001); Rita Nakashima Brock and Rebecca Ann Parker, *Proverbs of Ashes: Violence,*

Redemptive Suffering, and the Search for What Saves Us (Boston: Beacon, 2002).

5. See Rev. 3:16.

6. Audre Lorde, *Sister Outsider: Essays and Speeches* (Freedom, Calif.: Crossing, 1984), 54.

7. Ibid., 59.

8. Ibid., 57.

9. Reinhold Niebuhr, *Moral Man and Immoral Society* (New York: Scribner's, 1960), 277.

10. Thomas Hoyt Jr., "Testimony," in Dorothy C. Bass, ed., *Practicing Our Faith: A Way of Life for a Searching People* (San Francisco: Jossey-Bass, 1997), 92, 102.

11. See Rosetta Ross, "From Civil Rights to Civic Participation," *Journal of the Interdenominational Theological Center* 28/1 (fall 2000/spring 2001): 2, and Rosetta E. Ross, *Witnessing and Testifying: Black Women, Religion, and Civil Rights* (Minneapolis: Fortress Press, 2003).

12. J. H. O'Dell, "Life in Mississippi: An Interview with Fannie Lou Hamer," *Freedomways* 5 (1965): 232; Phyl Garland, "Builders of a New South," *Ebony* 21 (August 1966): 28.

13. Fannie Lou Hamer, Foreword to *Stranger at the Gates: A Summer in Mississippi*, by Tracy Sugarman (New York: Hill and Wang, 1967), viii.

14. Fannie Lou Hamer, "Fannie Lou Hamer Speaks Out," *Essence* 1/6 (October 1971): 78.

15. Ross, *Witnessing and Testifying*, 109–10.

16. Hamer, "Fannie Lou Hamer Speaks Out," 75.

17. Susan Kling, *Fannie Lou Hamer: A Biography* (Chicago: Women for Racial and Economic Equality, 1979), 20.

18. Howell Raines, *My Soul Is Rested: Movement Days in the Deep South Remembered* (New York: Penguin, 1983), 254; Kling, *Fannie Lou Hamer*, 23.

7. The Passion and African American Pilgrimage

1. Robert M. Franklin, "Black Theology and the Passion," *Sightings*, February 19, 2004.

2. John Hope Franklin and Alfred A. Moss Jr., *From Slavery to Freedom: A History of African Americans*, 8th ed. (Boston: McGraw-Hill, 2000).

3. My discussion of cultural classics is indebted to the lectures of David Tracy and Martin Marty in an extraordinary course titled "Public Religion and Public Theology," which I took as a doctoral student at the University of Chicago Divinity School in 1980.

4. David Tracy, *Plurality and Ambiguity: Hermeneutics, Religion, Hope*, repr. ed. (Chicago: University of Chicago Press, 1994 [1987]), 12.

5. Gayraud S. Wilmore, *Black Religion and Black Radicalism: An Interpretation of the Religious History of African Americans*, 3rd ed., rev. and enl. (Maryknoll, N.Y.: Orbis, 1998).

6. Martin Luther King Jr., *Strength to Love* (Philadelphia: Fortress Press, 1981 [1963]).

CPSIA information can be obtained at www.ICGtesting.com
Printed in the USA
LVOW11s0425180715

446699LV00017B/168/P